Washington State's
ROUND BARNS

Preserving a Vanishing Rural Heritage

WASHINGTON STATE'S
ROUND
BARNS

Tom Bartuska and Helen Bartuska

Pam Overholtzer, Editor

BASALT
BOOKS

Pullman, Washington

BASALT BOOKS

Basalt Books
PO Box 645910
Pullman, Washington 99164-5910
Phone: 800-354-7360
Email: basalt.books@wsu.edu
Website: basaltbooks.wsu.edu

Library of Congress Cataloging-in-Publication Data

Names: Bartuska, Tom J., author. | Bartuska, Helen, author.
Title: Washington state's round barns : preserving a vanishing rural
   heritage / Tom Bartuska and Helen Bartuska ; Pam Overholtzer, editor.
Description: Pullman, Washington : Basalt Books, [2024] | Includes
   bibliographical references and index.
Identifiers: LCCN 2023057971 | ISBN 9781638640240 (paperback) | ISBN
   9781638640271 (hardback)
Subjects: LCSH: Round barns--Washington (State)--Guidebooks. | Washington
   (State)--Guidebooks. | BISAC: ARCHITECTURE / Adaptive Reuse & Renovation
   | ARCHITECTURE / Buildings / Public, Commercial & Industrial
Classification: LCC NA8230 .B29 2024 | DDC 728/.92209797--dc23/eng/20240103
LC record available at https://lccn.loc.gov/2023057971

Images presented in this volume were taken by the authors unless otherwise indicated.
Frontispiece: Steptoe Butte, Washington. Image by the authors.

Basalt Books is an imprint of Washington State University Press.

The Washington State University Pullman campus is located on the homelands of the Niimíipuu (Nez Perce) Tribe and the Palus people. We acknowledge their presence here since time immemorial and recognize their continuing connection to the land, to the water, and to their ancestors. WSU Press is committed to publishing works that foster a deeper understanding of the Pacific Northwest and the contributions of its Native peoples.

Cover image: The Leonard Barn, by Janet Fry Photography
Cover design by Jeffry E. Hipp

CONTENTS

DEDICATION

We dedicate this book to the preservation of unique barns, buildings and communities which enhance the beauty of our rural landscape and cultural heritage. We are indebted to those discussed above and throughout this book, including our future readers, who are motivated to help preserve our past while creating a sustainable future.

We also dedicate this work to some very special people and companions in our life: Don, David, Jill, Jon, Dorian, Trish, Si, Quimby, Elfreda, Nimbus and Puff. They all have helped enrich our life's journey.

Thank you and our love. M&D/T&H

Robert Hubner, WSU Photo Services

Robert Hubner, WSU Photo Services

ACKNOWLEDGMENTS

First and foremost, we want to thank all the barn owners and their families for sharing their stories, allowing us to visit and photograph their barns. Many of these wonderful experiences are embedded in the story of the barns discussed in this book. We appreciate being able to document the twenty-one unique round barns in the State of Washington as well as a selected few out of many throughout this country. We also humbly thank the people who have had the will and wisdom to restore or reanimate the beauty of the barns, buildings and rural communities.

Secondly, we are also grateful for our editor, Pamela Overholtzer. Her professionalism in editing, word processing, design and formatting our manuscript was simply amazing and an important part of this work. Equally important, her extensive knowledge and experience in architecture and historic preservation fostered an effective collaboration. We could not have completed this project without her.

After residing and being educators for 40 years in Pullman, Washington, and Tom teaching at Washington State University, it is indeed an honor to have WSU Press further improve, design, and publish this book. We are grateful for the historical information and technical help from Michael Houser and Greg Griffish of the Washington State Department of Archaeology and Historic Preservation and Gayle O'Hara and others in the Manuscripts, Archives, and Special Collections (MASC) office at Washington State University for photographs and manuscripts. Also, equally important to our research was the wonderful help we received from various history museums of the communities where the barns were located. We appreciate the help of Jim Waddell and Steve Nys, Washington State University architecture graduates, for their involvement in restoring barns and suggestions to investigate others. Jim's effective leadership as the director of Pullman's Main Street Program was instrumental in reanimating its historic downtown. We want to acknowledge Rob Wagoner and Curtis Hughes for their assistance in photography and design throughout this project.

Besides the names noted above, we are very appreciative of past architecture students, family, and friends who have helped us discover and document many of the round barns as well as encouraging us along this journey.

Lastly, we also acknowledge with deep appreciation our planet Earth. We are very concerned about the disastrous effects of global warming and the massive impact it is having on the earth's cycles. Natural cycles are fundamental for growing food and for the trees that supplied the lumber for the barns and buildings. Embedded in this book is a plea to preserve our past while facing the challenges of our future. A century ago, the demand for these vital materials and energy resources was more sustainable; we hope they will be again in the future. To ensure the publishing of our book is carbon neutral, we will have The Arbor Day Foundation plant one tree for every book sold.

Robert Hubner, WSU Photo Services

Palouse landscape from Kamiak Butte.

CHAPTER I

Round Barns in the United States

Oh, dear barns, some rectangular, some round.

Their enhancement of our rural landscape is oh so profound.

Barns built over many generations will leave their mark. Their history continues to captivate the heart.

They have provided livelihood for families and farms,

While standing for centuries with beauty, strength and charm.

Their stories abound and await to be told. Intriguing, hidden mysteries; old, yet so bold.

Many have been lost from wind, snow and rain, while others are maintained and do still remain.

Farm markets form communities and the societal needs they serve. All important parts of the rural cultural heritage we must preserve.

Figure I.1: United States postcard stamps featuring barns, 2021–2022.

Why round barns and forms? Why are they so special? Why write about them?

All barns are important contributors to our agrarian history as well as icons of the beauty in the rural landscapes. Round barns, however, are especially intriguing; not only do they stand out wherever they are found, but they also hold a special place in our culture that exemplifies many related advancements in agricultural development. As they disappear and become "rural ruins," a great deal of our heritage, as well as much beauty in the country's landscape, is being lost.

We have personally been interested in round barns for over sixty years. We define "round" as a generalized term that includes polygon-shaped barns. During our long interest and curiosity about round barns, we have discovered an abundance of fascinating information about them, some interesting facts and many more stories. As we investigate and learn more about them, we are continually reminded of a profound sentiment from the naturalist, John Muir: *if you try to pick out anything by itself, you will find it connected to everything else in the Universe.* By picking out round barns while venturing down those various avenues of information (and related country lanes), we have discovered many personal, ecological, and cultural interconnections that we hope to convey in this work.

Round barns are special; they are disappearing and being lost due to changes in economics, technology as well as disrepair and climatic elements. We hope this work will ripple outward and inspire others to join in the effort to learn about and save these structures tucked away in the rural landscapes.

During our search, we have compared many resources and noted that no one, single inventory includes all the known round barns we have discovered to date in the state of Washington (Figure I.2). We have done our best to make this summary factual, but much comes from second-hand comments and stories. As time has passed, verification has become difficult: unfortunately, some

Figure I.2: Photo collage of some of the round barns found throughout the state of Washington. Out of the twenty-one barns we found, fourteen still stand.

of the people we contacted have passed away. We have endeavored to convey the essence of their information as accurately as possible.

We write this summary to encourage others to update, clarify and add to the story. Furthermore, we hope this work will help establish an appreciation of the barns in the state of Washington and, hopefully, more dialogue will follow to enrich the importance of these structures, clarify their history, and encourage repairs to preserve those that remain. They patiently await renewal and appropriate use or reuse. They are icons to the creativity and the beauty of Washington state's rural landscape.

Round Forms

An important and special aspect of this essay deals with an appreciation of the character of circular shapes and spherical forms. They are organic, a delight to the eye and mind, and each is a one-of-a-kind creation. They occur throughout nature as well as in our culture and the built environment from buildings and buttons, domes and drums, symbols and spider webs, teepees and totem poles, wheels, wedding rings and windmills… they are even found in the growth rings of trees (Figure I.3). In addition, the definition of a sphere is equally challenging, related and profound:

> Sphere: (from the Latin) circuit or range of action, knowledge or influence; natural, normal or proper place; the area over which something acts, exerts influence, has its being or significance.

As above, circles and spheres are synonymous with *cycles*: a fundamental part of life's supportive ecological systems that are so important to appreciate and understand, especially as we face the challenges of human-caused global warming. Like the carbon to oxygen cycle provided by plants and trees, many of these cycles are invisible but fundamental to life on Earth. The essential nutrient cycle is equally critical. As we know, yet sometimes forget, *all* *food* comes from these critical ecological cycles and the Earth's natural systems (and not from the grocery store). Barns are a vital part of this ecological cycle: they facilitate the efficient birth, production, growth, health and maintenance of the animals and plants that are so vital for human sustenance and health, and they reside at the core of the human food production system. As in all complete cycles, even human and plant wastes need to be composted and returned to enrich the soil and grow another nutrient/ food cycle—all facilitated by barns. A round barn, because of this cyclical connection, fulfills these functions even more seamlessly.

Ralph Waldo Emerson said,

> *The eye is the first circle; the horizon…is the second; and throughout nature this primary picture is repeated without end. It is the highest emblem in the cipher of the world. Our life is an apprenticeship to the truth that around every circle another can be drawn.*

Figure I.3: Photo collage of natural and human-created round patterns and forms.

The History and Development of Round Barns

Round barns are the human expression of that intimate connection between spheres and natural cycles expressed by an infinite number of circles found everywhere in nature. The question now, and the challenge before us, is: how does one unravel the special subject of round barns before they disappear and become rural ruins?

Most of the available literature states that the first renowned round barn was built by one of our nation's founders: it was designed by George Washington in 1792 and completed in 1794 (Figures I.4 and I.5). It is a 52-foot-diameter, sixteen-sided, two-story restored barn located at Washington's Dogue Run Farm in Fairfax County, Virginia,

designed specifically for efficient grain thrashing.[1]

Some interesting connections can be made here. First, the state of Washington is, of course, named after our country's first president, George Washington, the designer and owner of the nation's first round barn. Also, the town name of Colfax (in Washington) is a name quite similar to Fairfax (in Virginia). Colfax is the county seat of Whitman County, Washington, where the largest concentration of round barns in the state was built.

Another noteworthy round barn, made of stone, was built in 1826 at what is now the Hancock Shaker Village in Pittsfield, Massachusetts (Figures I-6 and I-7).[2] Most available literature on round barns states that the Hancock barn is the first influential round barn in the country. Shaker

communities emphasized simplicity and functional efficiency and probably appreciated not only the material savings of constructing round barns, but also the effective way of feeding the dairy cows from a central position. Both issues are discussed further in the next section. The Hancock barn is almost twice as large as the George Washington barn (95 feet in diameter) and was also built against a hill with a ramp to allow efficient access for hay carts to the second level loft for feed storage. The original barn burned down in 1864, probably due to a lack of proper ventilation (resulting in internal combustion). The barn was reconstructed with the upper clerestory ring and a vented cupola centrally located at the highest point on the roof. One story about the building of round barns is a Shaker legend that

Figures I.4 and I.5: The George Washington Barn at Dogue Run Farm in Fairfax County, Virginia, exterior (left) and interior.

evil spirits hide in corners; a building without corners would then eliminate such negative influences. (We wonder if that same reasoning applies to the rotundas in state and federal capitol buildings?) There surely must exist many earlier round barns, but they have not survived on the land or in the literature. The era when many round and polygon barns were built occurred between 1870 and 1920, although in Washington state most were constructed between 1890 and 1920, the beginning of the era of scientific agricultural research and publication. The reasons for constructing some of the earlier examples (1870–1880) are not clear, but, in some barns, there is reference to the George Washington and/or Hancock barns.

There is also an interesting relationship to the inherent qualities of Native American teepees, hogans, and yurts. They are, of course, round and, like circular barns, they enclose the greatest amount of interior space with the least amount of exterior material and construction. Also, round forms are more structurally stable than rectangular construction and create effective ventilation through the apex, which is critical to agricultural buildings.

The University of Illinois was one of the prominent land-grant universities, which did extensive scientific research and publishing on the effectiveness and efficiency of round barns. Land-grant universities, as institutions of higher education, are designated by each state's

Figures I.6 and I.7: The exterior (left) and interior of the Round Stone Barn at Hancock Shaker Village in Pittsfield, Massachusetts.

government to receive the benefits of the Morrill Acts of 1862 and 1890.

The mission of these institutions as set forth in the 1862 Act is to focus on the teaching of practical agriculture, science, military science, and engineering…as a response to the industrial revolution and changing social class. This mission was in contrast to the historic practice of higher education to focus on an abstract liberal arts curriculum.

The nation's oldest and original corn research plot still stands in the south center of that campus today. The plot, established in 1876, is named after George Morrow, a professor and dean of agriculture at the university (Figure I.8). Agricultural production has increased many times over the years in part due to the important research that has been conducted here.

The University of Illinois built three round barns of varying diameters

specifically to conduct scientific research to increase the efficiency of dairy farming (Figure I.9). The objectives were to improve sanitation and circulation, increase efficiency at minimal cost to the farmer, and improve dairy herds and the volume of production.

The first round barn was a 60-foot diameter barn built in 1908 (Figure I.9, barn on the right); the second was another 60-foot barn built in 1910 (Figure I.9, middle); and the third was a 70-foot diameter barn built in 1912 (Figure I.9, left; also pictured in Figure I-10). The three University of Illinois barns are on the National Register of Historic Places and still stand today, gracing the rural landscape on the edge of campus.

The publishing of various agricultural bulletins helped disseminate their promising findings about the efficiency of round barns to the farming communities. A major summary report

titled *Economy of the Round Dairy Barn* published in February 1910 had a major influence on the increased development of round barns throughout the nation. The UI research publication stated:

The sole objective being to produce the largest amount of milk per acre at the least possible cost. To meet the requirements of a barn for this purpose, it became imperative to build one that was convenient for feeding and caring for cows, economical of construction and containing a large storage capacity in both the silo and mow.[3]

The bulletin discussed in detail the functional efficiency, structural stability, unique radial framing (Figures I.11 and I.12), effective ventilation, construction, and cost effectiveness of these experimental round barns. The circular plan allowed efficient feeding of the animals via a central location from a silo and/or the second level hayloft or

THE MORROW PLOTS
AMERICA'S OLDEST EXPERIMENTAL FIELD
ESTABLISHED IN 1876
RESULTS DEMONSTRATE THAT USE OF
SCIENCE AND TECHNOLOGY
HAS INCREASED CROP PRODUCTIVITY
OVER FOUR-FOLD.

Figure I.8: The Morrow Plots, the oldest experimental field in the United States, have been growing corn for nearly 150 years.

Figure I.9: Aerial image of the three University of Illinois round experimental barns. (Google Maps)

Figure I.10: One of the three University of Illinois round experimental barns, 70 feet in diameter (shown on the left side of the aerial photo in Figure I.9). The dairy cows are cared for on the lower level and the hay and silage are brought in on the upper level.

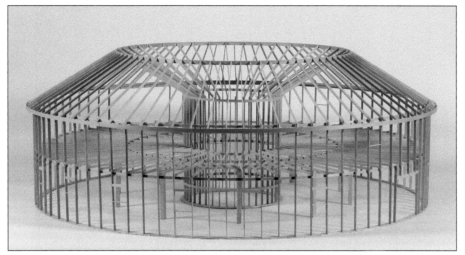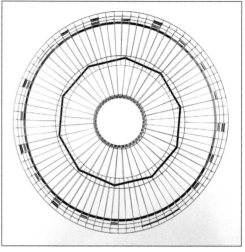

Figures I.11 and I.12: Model (left) and aerial perspective of the intricate, radial wood framing of the Jim Kaney Round Barn, Aledine, Illinois, built in 1905. The Kaney Barn design is unique, as the inner circular segment—usually a silo supporting a dome roof—is actually concave and funnels rainwater for the animals. This model was on display at the Architecture and Design Museum in Palm Springs, California in spring 2023, and was featured as one of ten models in an international exhibition on the importance of wood framing in the development of the United States. Images courtesy of American Framing.

"mow" (Figures I.13 and I.14). Like the Hancock barn, they had a ramp to the second level for easy unloading of horse-drawn carts. The circular shape also allowed the carts to circle around without having to back up (similar to the way a cul-de-sac or traffic circle functions). Detailed plans, framing diagrams and construction photographs were enticingly presented to the reader. A close correlation exists between the dates of these agricultural publications and the sizes and layouts of many round and polygon barns subsequently built throughout the country, including those in the state of Washington.

An interesting aspect of the UI research was a careful comparative analysis of the cost of materials of the round barn versus the cost of materials for an equally sized rectangular one. The report included a detailed list of materials for each. (See Figure I.15, top: Table 2A—A Comparison of the Cost on Material in Round and Rectangular Barns.) At the time, building materials were the major expense of a barn's construction; in most cases, labor was not as significant because most barns were built by extended families and shared labor from

neighbors. Today, labor tends to be a major cost factor in construction that is usually at least equal to, if not more expensive than, the materials needed to build a structure. Accommodating for inflation, a $10 material purchased in 1910 would cost $293.02 in 2023.[4] (See Figure I.15, bottom: Table 2B.) As stated in the report based on those 1910 costs, the total savings in materials for a 60-foot-diameter round barn versus an equivalent sized rectangular barn (plank framing) was $426.50, for a cost savings of 36 percent. The larger 90-foot-diameter barn versus the comparable-sized rectangular (plank framing) barn was $781.62 less, or a 34 percent savings. In 2023 dollars, the approximate cost savings would be $11,682 and $21,411, respectively, for the two sizes of barns—a significant amount of money for any farmer, especially during the late 1800s and early 1900s.

Besides original construction techniques that could be challenging, the primary disadvantage in the round barns was expansion. The two sizes—60 feet and the proposed 90 feet developed in the UI research—were considered optimum sizes for a profitable and

efficient family dairy farm with 1900-era technology. As technology advanced, a farming family could manage larger numbers of cows, and the fixed capacity of the circular form limited expansion. Consequently, many round barns had rectangular additions added to them. The 70- and 80-foot diameter barns then became more popular, because they allowed for the efficiency of the 60-foot barn but had an expanded ring for more cows and increased storage in the loft.

Paralleling the land-grant university's research were architects and engineers such as Benton Steele and William Louden who specialized in barn construction (Figures I.16–18). Steele, residing in Indiana and later relocating to Kansas, was considered "the Frank Lloyd Wright of round barns." He stated in various advertisements "Round Barns are the cheapest and best from every standpoint" and "My Specialty is Rural Architecture. The Round Barn is my hobby." He designed and built many barns throughout the Midwest, including the three University of Illinois barns. William Louden established the Louden Manufacturing Company, an engineering,

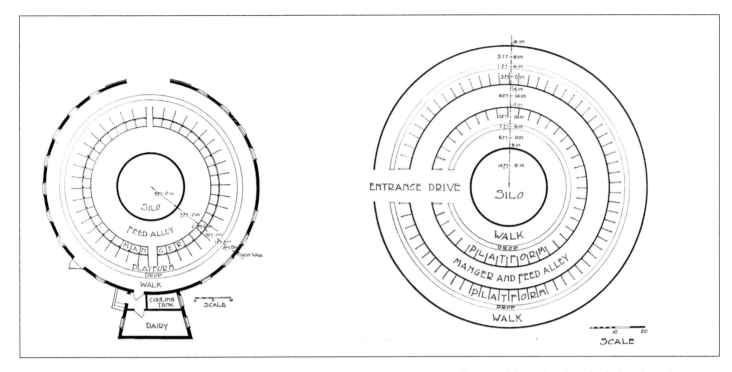

Figures I.13 and I.14: Plans for the 60-foot barn (left) and a proposed 90-foot barn. Note the efficiency of the 60-foot barn for feeding from the central silo and milking by the daylight from the perimeter windows.

TABLE 2A.—A COMPARISON OF THE COST OF MATERIAL IN ROUND AND RECTANGULAR BARNS, *Including* FOUNDATION AND SILOS.

	Round barn, 60 feet in diameter	Rectangular barn, 36 x 78½ ft.	
		Plank frame	Mortise frame
Lumber in barn,	$799 76	$1023.27	$1233.41
Material in foundation,	86.89	105.90	105.90
Material in silo,	159.01	295.26	295.26
Total cost of material in barn,	**$1045.66**	**$1424.43**	**$1634.57**
Actual money saved,		**$378.77**	**$588.91**
Proportional cost,	**100%**	**136%**	**156%**

TABLE 2B.

	Round barn, 90 feet in diameter	Rectangular barn, 36 x 176¾ ft.	
		Plank frame	Mortise frame
Lumber in barn,	$1628.48	$2007.67	$2497.56
Material in foundation,	130.35	196.80	196.80
Material in silo,	265.00	513.52	513.52
Total cost of material in barn,	**$2023.83**	**$2717.99**	**$3207.88**
Actual money saved,		**$694.16**	**$1184.05**
Proportional cost,	**100%**	**134%**	**158%**

Figure I.15: Tables 2A and 2B from a 1910 University of Illinois report comparing the material costs of round and rectangular barns.

Figure I.16: Benton Steele's advertisement for round barn plans.

Figures I.17 and I.18: Louden's barn plans publication, left, and an interior page featuring a round barn.

manufacturing, and design company. In 1906, Louden began its architecture department, developed various publications and stock plans of various barns, and designed more than 25,000 from 1906 to 1939. The company's publications included round barns (Figures I.17 and I.18). The Radford Company also published barn plans in 1909.[5]

Along with the Louden Company, the popular Sears, Roebuck catalog sold kits for round barns (Figure I.19). The kits included pre-cut lumber, roof shingles, hardware, windows, and even enough paint for two coats of the structure. Kit number 2071, offered in 1918, was for a 60-foot diameter, 48-foot-tall round barn with cypress siding. The kit cost $1,627.[6] Cypress was one of the most durable woods available at that time and is rather expensive now. In reference to the cost today, $1,627 would be $27,973.22—still an amazing bargain.

From 1880 to 1920, Washington state experienced exponential population growth, expansion, and prosperity in agriculture. The completion of the transcontinental railroads linking the Pacific Northwest with the rest of the United States was the single most important factor contributing to this growth.[7] Many who migrated to Washington came from the more settled eastern and central regions of the United States and arrived with "modern" ideas in farming and plans to purchase farmland (and, potentially, an interest in building a round barn).

A Land-Grant University, Prototype Round Barns, Event Centers, and a Museum

We—the authors of this volume—met when we were in high school. We both lived west of Chicago in Berwyn, Illinois, and we later attended the University of Illinois Urbana-Champaign, one of the nation's first land-grant institutions. We remember the rural beauty of UI's round prototype barns on the campus. Helen's major was home economics, child and family studies, while Tom studied architecture and learned about the special qualities of round forms used around the world throughout history: indigenous teepees, kivas, and hogans, along with the great domes of cathedrals, mosques, government buildings, and important gathering places. The round Foellinger Auditorium located at the center of the University of Illinois served a significant role on campus: it was the meeting place for important events that included world-renowned speakers, concerts, and educational and cultural activities (Figure I.20). Also located on campus was a massive round arena, the Assembly Hall (later renovated and renamed the State Farm Center), commonly referred to as "the flying saucer," which served as the venue for many large campus cultural and sporting events (Figure I.21). The dome, completed in 1963, is 400 feet in diameter and has a seating capacity of over 15,000.

The state of Washington had a similar but larger round event center—the Kingdome. The huge concrete building, completed in 1976, had a 660-foot-diameter with seating capacity for 40,000 to 66,000. It was imploded in 2000 to make room for a new Seahawks and Sounders stadium, currently known as Lumen Field.[8] The Kingdome drew its name from King County, which was named in honor of Martin Luther King, Jr. Seattle itself was named for a

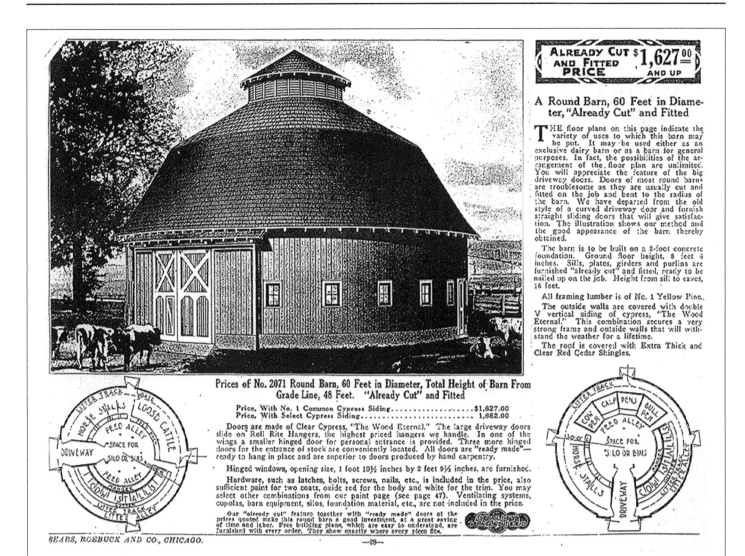

Figure I.19: An ad for a 60-foot-diameter round barn construction kit available from the Sears, Roebuck catalog in 1919.

compassionate Native American leader, Chief Si'ahl, who helped people settle in the region while caring deeply about the earth and all who dwelled upon it. It is important to note that Seattle was wise to locate the Kingdome and their newer sport stadiums adjacent to the downtown and close to public transportation, reinforcing an active center and minimizing auto-driven sprawl.

The state has a similarly large round event center: the Tacoma Dome (Figures I.22 and I.23).[9] This structure is 530 feet in diameter, 152 feet in height, and has a seating capacity of 21,000. It

Figures I.20 and I.21: On the left, the University of Illinois' Foellinger Auditorium rotunda, and the "flying saucer" arena (now named the State Farm Center), in Champaign, Illinois.

Figures I.22 and I.23: On the left, the Tacoma Dome with Mt. Rainer in the background, and, right, the dome's interior during a sporting event. Photographs courtesy of Western Wood Structures, Inc.

is the largest wood geodesic dome by volume in the world.[10] Built in 1983, it was designed by Tacoma architects McGranahan and Messenger, who were the winners of an international competition. The wood used to build the massive roof came from trees blown down in the 1980 eruption of Mount St. Helens. Another round event center, the Superior Dome in Marquette, Michigan, is 6 feet larger in diameter but is only 143 feet high with a seating capacity of 16,000.[11]

Detroit, Michigan, is home to another contemporary building with a beautiful round atrium: the Wright Museum for African American History (Figures I.24 and I.25). It was built in 1997 and has one of the largest collections of African-American cultural artifacts in the world.[12] The museum was designed by architects Sims-Varner.

Their inspiration featured a round form based upon traditional African buildings.[13] The central circular atrium, or rotunda, is 100 feet in diameter and 55 feet high to the top of its glass dome. The size is similar to that of large round barns and it emulates, in contemporary ways, the inherent spatial and structural qualities of the handcrafted, wooden round barns that are discussed in the next two chapters.[14]

Figures I.24 and I.25: The exterior (left) and interior of the Wright Museum of African American History in Detroit, Michigan. Photographs courtesy of the Wright Museum of African American History.

A Brief Personal Story and the History of Pullman, Washington

We moved to Pullman, Washington in 1963, when Tom accepted a teaching position in architecture at Washington State University, also a land-grant institution with prominent agriculture, science and engineering colleges. The town of Pullman had some intriguing parallels with Illinois. Pullman was originally called Three Forks, a charming name, selected after the early settlers built in a valley at the confluence of three streams. By 1884, the town leaders devised a plan to rename the growing community in the hopes of attracting more development. The story goes that they turned to wealthy industrialist George Pullman. He was the inventor of the Pullman railroad car, developer of the new planned community of Pullman, Illinois, and builder of an extensive manufacturing facility also located there. If they renamed their town after him, they hoped it would engender his enthusiastic support and possibly a major regional transportation center or manufacturing facility. It is commonly believed that George Pullman showed his appreciation for his namesake town by sending $50 worth of banners and artifacts for the renaming celebration. Whether the story is true or not, his gift was considerably less than the town fathers had envisioned.

By 1891, Pullman had attracted the attention of the state, which was looking to locate its land-grant institution on a 160-acre site northwest of the town. The college, first named Washington Agricultural College and School of Science, opened to 59 students in 1892. In 1905, it was renamed State College of Washington, or Washington State College, and in 1959 it became Washington State University (WSU).

WSU is located in the beautiful Palouse region of eastern Washington. The Palouse, possibly named after either the Palus Indigenous Tribe or a French word for "grass lands," is a stunning landscape of rolling, treeless hills dotted with small agricultural communities, farms, and the largest number of round barns in the state. The fertile soil developed into productive wheat and legumes farmland, adding to the picturesque landscape as the rolling wheat fields changed with the seasons from snow white, to spring green, to harvest gold in the summer and fall. The Palouse region is illustrated and discussed on pages 32–56. In addition, the annual National Lentil Festival is held in Pullman—it is discussed in more detail on page 182.

For us, Pullman and the Palouse were an ideal environment to live, work, and play while continuing our love affair with round patterns, circular barns, rural landscapes, and communities. As a Montessori teacher, Helen used circles for discussions, sharing, and singing as an enjoyable and constructive time in her teaching. When a child had a birthday, the class had a special celebration in which the children would sit in a circle around a lighted candle (symbolizing the sun), and the birthday child would carry a ball (a replica of the earth) and walk around the "sun" singing a special song.

On Tom's part, he found teaching was most effective in discussion circles. He continually emphasized that we are all part of, and interdependent with, ecological cycles and encouraged his students to design with "nature"—both human and environmental nature. At times, he was able to interweave his interest in round barns into his teaching of architecture and planning. When discussing vernacular (or regional) architecture, he often asked if the students knew of any round barns, and in some cases he engaged their interest enough to carry out research projects on these special structures. They added to our collective knowledge while helping to create our comprehensive inventory of round barns throughout the state. Pullman and WSU are further explored in Chapter IV.

The following list includes some excellent publications on historic round barns in other states:

Hanou, J. *Round Indiana: Round Barns in the Hoosier State.* Purdue University Press, 1993.

Jackson, J. *Stories from the Round Barn.* TriQuarterly Press, 2000.

Jackson, J. *The Round Barn: A Biography of the American Farm* (four volumes). University of Chicago Press, 2013.

Kanfer, L and A. *Barns of Illinois.* University of Illinois Press, 2009.

Soike, L. *Without Right Angles: The Round Barns of Iowa.* Iowa Department of General Services, 1983.

Triumpho, R. *Round Barns of New York.* Syracuse University Press, 2004.

Twiggs, J. *Keeping the Barn.* Montana PBS, 2020.

Wizowaty, S. *The Round Barn.* University Press of New England, 2002.

NOTES

1. George Washington Barn. http://en.wikipedia.org/wiki/Round_barn and http://www.mountvernon.org/digital-encyclopedia/article/16-sided-barn/

2. https://en.wikipedia.org/wiki/Hancock_Shaker_Village and http://en.wikipedia.org/wiki/Land-grant_university

3. Fraser, W. *Economy of the Round Dairy Barn.* Agricultural Bulletin No 143, February 1910, University of Illinois Agricultural Experiment Station (Champaign, Illinois, February 1910).

4. CBI Inflation Calculator online. www.calculator.net-financial

5. *Radford Book of Barn Plans.* Radford Company. 1909

6. Nizalowski, E. "The Sears Barn in Newark Valley, NY." The Barn Journal website www.thebarnjournal.org/stories/story012/

7. https://en.wikipedia.org/wiki/State_Farm_Center

8. https://en.wikipedia.org/wiki/Kingdome

9. https://en.wikipedia.org/wiki/Tacoma_Dome

10. http://westernwoodstructures.blogspot.com/2012/08/ the-tacoma-dome.html

11. National Register of Historic Places. OMB No 10240018, Section E (U.S. Department of the Interior, National Park Service, Washington, DC) p. 11.

12. https://en.wikipedia.org/wiki/Charles_H._Wright_Museum_of_African_American_History

13. https://www.thewright.org/visit

14. https://sah-archipedia.org/buildings/MI-01-WN66

Vineyards on Bainbridge Island, Washington, with cornfields in the distance.

Robert Hubner, WSU Photo Services

CHAPTER II

The Twenty-one Round Barns in Washington State

Aristotle believed the sphere was the most "perfect" of shapes. This implies there is a special purpose for a round barn. It is efficient for human labor, organic in form, beautiful to the eye, and represents life-sustaining cycles in nature.

The Leonard Barn within the Palouse landscape. Photo courtesy of Ken Carper.

There were twenty-one historic round barns in the state of Washington known to us. Of these twenty-one, two have burned down, four have collapsed or were removed due to weather damage (rain, wind, and heavy snowstorms), and one was taken down to make way for suburban development. We are hopeful that the remaining fourteen will be maintained, restored, and preserved, and that this publication might inspire those who would preserve them. Some barns have been well cared for, but others will need help if they are to survive in the landscape. We will discuss examples of round barns that have been preserved in other states and other related structures in Chapters III and IV.

Please note that many other round structures are used for agricultural functions. We have limited this work to large historic barns—defined as those structures over 50 years old, with two or more stories and over 50 feet in diameter. The following is a generally chronological listing of the barns—the oldest of those built in 1872—and several have been grouped together due to common locations (e.g., barns 3, 4, 5, 6 and 7 are all located on the Palouse. See list on page 17, and map on pages 18–19). We have included all the round barns we are aware of, and we include those that we know were built but which no longer exist. Please note the symbols used for each barn: ● signifies existing round barns, ⬣ signifies existing polygon barns, and ◆ represents those that have disappeared from the rural landscape but remain in our memories, photographs, and literature. We have endeavored to research each barn, but our essays vary in content due to the often limited resources available to us.

We encourage the reader to appreciate the deeply embedded symbiotic ecological cycles (human and natural) in building these amazing barns in the late 1800s and early 1900s—particularly the ingenuity of constructing such large structures using hand-crafted tools and the technology of that time. For most structures, family and neighbors collaborated on the construction of the barns, forming a communal bond and pride in their shared labor and accomplishments.

This symbiotic cycle began with the trees: many builders used logs harvested directly from their property or from adjacent forests. Some builders used round, un-milled timber when possible, especially for structural support. As our symbiotic partners, trees (and by extension all plants) are vital in combating global warming by absorbing carbon dioxide (CO_2) from the atmosphere. In a general sense, wood is the embodied carbon from all living creatures, including humans and our extensive use of fossil fuels. Unfortunately, today we do not have enough trees in our environment to absorb the huge amounts of CO_2 being released into the atmosphere. Therefore, saving our barns not only retains the beauty of our rural cultural heritage, but it also prevents the release of the stored carbon until such time as the structure is destroyed (burned or left to decay). This topic is further discussed in Chapter IV.

Parallel to the construction of these barns in the early 1900s was the Arts and Crafts Movement. In brief, the Arts and Crafts Movement was inspired by nature and simpler, more traditional handcrafted design—a reaction to, and rejection of, the overly embellished detail of the Victorian era and the impersonal nature of industrialization. These barns epitomize the intent of the Movement, and arts and crafts are still honored today in many handmade objects (art, jewelry, writing, pottery, furniture, some family-built homes, and even traditional barns). For example, in Chapter IV we discuss the work of Jack Sobon's workshop to reconstruct a historic barn in Pullman, and the Smith straw bale home is discussed on pp. 143–45. Both stories exemplify the integrity of using natural materials and traditional handcrafted construction.

We have respected those owners who did not want their barns discussed in this volume. Some barns still seem to be a bit of a treasure waiting to be discovered, while most have a rich, rewarding, and wonderful story to tell.

As stated in the Acknowledgements, we are indebted for the help of the Washington State Department of Archeology and Historic Preservation (DAHP). Their Heritage Barn Register lists some 700 significant historic barns in the state's 39 counties. A unique part of this listing is nine of the existing round barns. In chronological order they are the Nutter Barn, built in 1872; the Laughlin Barn, 1883; the Seitz/Frazier Barn, 1903; the Marble Ranch Barn, 1914; the Steinke, Minnehaha/Ayers/McGraph, and the Crocker Barns, all from 1915; the Middleburg Barn, 1916; and the Leonard Barn, 1917. The DAHP and information in the register have helped to clarify the history of these nine barns. Of these barns, four also have listings in the National Register of Historic Places: the Laughlin Barn, the Marble Ranch Barn, the Steinke Barn, and the Leonard Barn. One additional property, the Coffman Barn, is included as part of a National Register historic district.

The Heritage Barn Register was created in 2007 to commemorate barns "as historically significant resources representing the agricultural, economic and cultural development of the state of Washington." In addition, DAHP provides significant matching grants for the registered barn owners "to support their efforts to preserve, stabilize and rehabilitate their barns." Parallel to our criteria, the barns must be at least 50 years old to qualify for such funding. The website for the DAHP Heritage Barn Register and programs is https://dahp.wa.gov/historic-registers/heritage-barn-register.

Chris Gregoire, the Washington state governor at the time of the Heritage Barn Register's inception, stated "Barns are a symbol of Washington's agricultural heritage and are beautiful buildings in their own right...The Heritage Barn Register will support the efforts of the Washingtonians who own these barns to preserve and stabilize these icons of our history."[1]

THE ROUND BARNS IN WASHINGTON STATE

1. ⬣ Nutter polygon barn, 1872

2. ● Laughlin/Kling/Selander round barn, 1883

Round Barns of Whitman County (the county with the highest number of round barns in Washington state)

3. ◆ Manning round barn, 1900–1953

4. ⬣ Steinke polygon barn, 1915

5. ◆ Hall Brothers' polygon barns: George Hall's barn, 1916–1985

6. ◆ Hall Brothers' polygon barns: Tom Hall's barn 1916–1979

7. ⬣ Leonard polygon barn, 1917

Round Barns Throughout Washington

8. ● Coffman round barn and carriage house, 1902

9. ⬣ and 10. ⬣ Seitz/Frazier polygon barns, 1903

11. ◆ Duskin round barn, 1916–1997

12. ◆ Wiester round barn, 1914–1981

13. ● Cornell/Marble Ranch round barn, 1916

14. ⬣ Minnehaha/Ayers/McGraph polygon barn, 1915

15. ⬣ Crocker Ranch polygon barn, 1915

16. ⬣ Hardin polygon barn, 1915

17. ⬣ Middleburg/Burge/Deep Creek round barn, 1916

18. ◆ Gallaher round barn, 1916–1920s

19. ● Yochum Ranch round barn, 1954

20. ⬣ Wagner polygon barn, 1971

21. ◆ Stewart half-polygon barn, 1914–1963

Nutter Barn, Cathlamet | p.21

Laughlin/Kling Barn, Castle Rock | p.27

Manning Barn, Pullman/Colfax | p.35

Stewart Barn, Mazama | p.107

Wagner Barn, Winthrop | p.103

Yochum Ranch Barn, Clarkston | p.99

Gallaher Barn, Mansfield | p.95

Middleburg/Burge Barn, Medical Lake | p.91

round barns still existing

polygon barns still existing

barns that have disappeared and become rural ruins

0   25   50 miles

0   25   50 kilometers

Hardin Barn, near Spokane | p.89

Crocker Ranch Barn, Centerville | p.85

Steinke Barn, St. John | p.39

George Hall Barn, Steptoe | p.45

Tom Hall Barn, Steptoe | p.45

Leonard Barn, Pullman | p.51

Coffman Barn, Chehalis | p.57

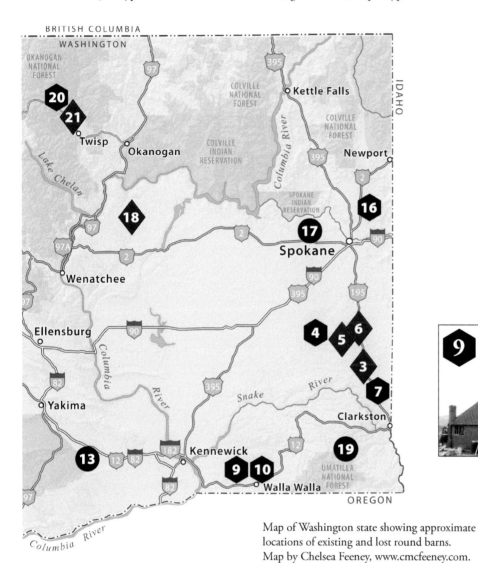

Map of Washington state showing approximate locations of existing and lost round barns. Map by Chelsea Feeney, www.cmcfeeney.com.

Seitz/Frazier Barns, Walla Walla | p.61

Duskin Barn, Arlington | p.65

Minnehaha/Ayers/McGraph Barn, Yakima | p.81

Marble Ranch Barn, Grandview | p.77

Weister Barn, Skamokawa | p.71

Recommendations when Visiting a Barn

Although we have found most barn owners to be very friendly and proud of their barns, we **strongly recommend** contacting the owners before planning to visit any of them. We have received information about contacting owners from the community's historic museums and societies. They have called the owners and then—**only** with their permission—provided their phone numbers. We will not give out any phone numbers.

Without permission from the barn owners, you may travel long distances, only to find the gates to the farm locked. It is imperative that you always obey "No Trespassing" signs and respect their right to privacy. Without permission, you may only see these great barns from public roads. If no restrictions are posted, **always** go directly to the home and kindly ask for information and permission to see the barn. If no one is

home, you should try making contact again another day and not access the barn. If the owner is home and access is allowed, be careful of animals—dogs, livestock, and if you're lucky, a barn owl. In most barns, the ground floor is likely dirt so it may be uneven and used for storage. **Be careful where you walk**. Also, you may see the loft through an opening from the ground floor. If allowed access to the loft, **be especially careful of the old ladders**. Also, some of the flooring in the loft may be uneven or weak, so test your footing when walking around. **You are obligated to take full responsibility for your adventure.**

As discussed previously, this project has been a collaborative process. If anyone has additional information about the history and location of round barns in the state of Washington, please forward it to us at tbartuska@wsu.edu.

Also, for those interested in a comprehensive survey of round barns, buildings, and covered bridges throughout the United States, we encourage you to explore Dale J. Travis's wonderful website: http://www.dalejtravis.com/. We carefully studied his inventory, and nine of the fourteen existing barns in Washington are listed. Some of the structures listed on his website did not meet our criteria for inclusion: having been used for agriculture, at least 50 years old, and a minumum of two stories. Many of the barns in his inventory are round one-story storage structures and buildings. We did discover several new barns, which are discussed in detail in the pages that follow. And as noted, we also offer a list of additional readings about round barns on page 12 and at the end of Chapter V, p. 187 at the back of this book.

Farm landscape near Dayton, Washington, with the Blue Mountains in the background.

1. Nutter Polygon Barn, 1872
(originally the Duthie Barn)

The Nutter Barn is the oldest known segmented octagonal barn (generally categorized as round) and the only round barn in the state to have been moved to a new location.

Original Location: 31-59 Greenwood Road, Cathlamet, Wahkiakum County, Washington

Current Location: 50 Forest Heights, Cathlamet, Wahkiakum County, Washington

Original use: Dairy and cattle barn without a silo in the center

Current use: Relocated; partially restored and used for storage

Characteristics: Octagonal plan with an eight-segmented, cone-shaped gable roof. It is sixty feet in diameter and was originally designed for dairy cows on the lower level with a hayloft on the second level.

The Nutter Barn is the oldest known "round" (polygon) barn in Washington. The original location was on a hill overlooking the town of Cathlamet and the Columbia River beyond (Figure II.1.1). Not a great deal is known about its original owner and builder, but it was partially restored after having been moved from its original location (Figures II.1.2–6). It currently stands in a field behind the Cathlamet cemetery (Figures II.1.7 and II.1.12).

Figure II.1.1: The Nutter (Duthie) Barn on its original hillside overlooking the Columbia River, 1980.

Figure II.1.2: The Nutter (Duthie) Barn in 1980. Note the stone foundation, an early construction method before the availability and popular use of concrete.

Figures II.1.3, II.1.4, and II.1.5: Top two images illustrate the second-level loft with radial octagon framing pattern. Bottom image shows the barn's ground level interior . Photos by H. Hatschek, 2007.

The State Historic Property Inventory Report states that the history of ownership of the property was thought to be a family named Strong and in 1847 the property was sold to Edward Haynes Watkins who had emigrated from England. The barn must have been built in 1872 by the Duthie family, as the historic name is known as the Duthie Barn. Ownership is unclear from that time forward until Lee Nutter purchased the barn and, in 2011–12, moved it to its current location and changed the name to The Nutter Barn.

The Nutter Barn, like some other early round and polygon barns, was built around a large live tree. After completion, the tree was removed. (See Figures II.1.3–4 and 8–11 showing roof framing). The unique aspect of this roof framing system is the eight main beams, which define the shape of the octagon roof segments and are the main supports extending from the eaves to the central tree stump—each one a massive, continuous timber 45 feet in length.[2]

When we visited the barn in 1980, the gentleman we spoke with at that time was quite enthusiastic about the barn and its history. When we revealed we were from Pullman and affiliated with WSU, he smiled and told us how Cathlamet had originally been in the running as a potential site for the location of the state's land-grant agriculture and engineering college (now WSU). We always find these types of connections intriguing. We wonder what our lives would have been like if the state's land-grant college had been located there and we had lived in the community of Cathlamet and surrounding Columbia River region rather than in the equally picturesque Palouse region surrounding Pullman. We could have been neighbors, sharing his pride in

Figure II.1.6: In 2011 the Nutter Barn was moved from its original site to its current location. Here it is shown sitting above the formwork for its new concrete foundation. Photo by H. Hatschek.

Figure II.1.7: Aerial view of the restored Nutter Barn in its new location, a pasture to the west of the Greenwood Cemetery. (Google Maps)

this historic town, the university, and, of course, this striking octagon barn.

In 2015, we revisited the barn at its new location and were delighted to see the restored barn sitting with the original rectilinear framing for the upper floor intact and the radial roof structure protected with a new metal roof (Figure II.1.12). The historic photographs of the barn, as well as the one on its new foundation, are by H. Hatschek from the Dale Travis website (Figures II.1.13–15).

Figure II.1.8: The upper loft of the restored Nutter Barn shows the beautiful radial octagonal framing of the roof.

Figures II.1.9, II.1.10, and II.1.11: Three photos of the barn's lower level, showing its rectilinear framing on its new concrete foundation. The original exterior siding was cedar board and batten. As shown in Figure II.1.8 and II.1.12 on p. 25 (showing exterior view), the battens have not been installed, creating a rather beautiful lighting condition for these interior photographs. If the battens are not installed, however, rain may cause significant water damage.

Figure II.1.12: The restored and relocated barn, with the same pastoral setting overlooking the Columbia River.

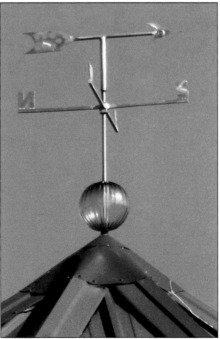

Figure II.1.15: An historic plaque located on the placed and restored barn, supported in part by the Washington State Department of Archaeology and Historic Preservation in association with the Heritage Barn Advisory Board.

Figure II.1.13: The original historic framing with hand-hewn timbers and dowel connections.

Figure II.1.14: A beautiful new weathervane and lightning rod sit atop the barn.

2. Laughlin/Kling/Selander Round Barn, 1883

This barn is the oldest known circular barn in the state and was substantially rebuilt after a storm in the 1980s.

Location: 9240 Barnes Drive, Castle Rock, Cowlitz County, Washington

Original use: Dairy barn with hayloft on the second floor

Current use: Farm implements and storage

Characteristics: The barn has a circular plan without a silo in the center. It is 63 feet in diameter with a cone-shaped gable roof and a T-shaped rectangular addition. It has a unique central column that branches out like an umbrella to hold up a ring for the roof beams and cupola.

The Laughlin Round Barn is generally considered to be the second oldest "round" barn in the state. However, since the Nutter Barn, built just one year earlier, is a segmented polygon shape, the Laughlin Barn can actually be considered the oldest *round* barn in the state (Figure II.2.1). The barn was built by Samuel D. Laughlin in 1883 on his family's 80-acre homestead (Figure II.2.2). It has a hand-hewn structural frame using on-site timbers. It has a one-of-a-kind central column connection support with twenty radial roof beams—one of the most beautiful central column support systems in the state (if not in the nation) (Figures II.2.3 and II.2.4). This unique radial

Figure II.2.1: The Laughlin Barn in 2015.

Figure II.2.2: Aerial view of the farm and barn. (Google Maps)

Figure II.2.3: Interior of the second-floor loft and beautiful central column in 2015.

structure is accented by light from the crowning cupola. Mr. Laughlin may have visited or been influenced by the round barn built in 1882 by Mr. French in Frenchglen, Oregon, which has a similar central column fanning out to support the roof framing. (See the Frenchglen Barn, pp.112–116.) Soon after Mr. Laughlin's death in 1910, the farm and barn were purchased by the Kling family.

By the 1980s, the barn had with-stood 100 years of rain, earthquakes, and major windstorms: a testimonial to Mr. Laughlin's skills and the structural strength of round forms. Mrs. Kling's love for this barn was instrumental in rebuilding it in the late 1980s. She, with the help of others, established the Cowlitz Round Barn Preservation Association[3] to maintain this barn she loved so much and find an alternative use. In 1986, the barn and property were sold to Tony and Alex Selander. They state that on their first night at the property, a major storm caused signifi-cant damage to the structure, inspiring

Figure II.2.4: The central column and radiating braces are beautifully accented by light from the crowning cupola.

them to join with Mrs. Kling to repair and rebuild the barn. Steve Nys, a Portland architect and former WSU student also interested in restoring historic buildings, did construction drawings to get the county to issue a building permit to restore this historic barn. (See the Leonard Barn, pp. 51–56, Figures II.7.9–11. Nys, along with another student, received a national award for their work.)

Patrick Wilkin's chapter "For Love of a Barn" in his book *Somewhere in the Northwest*[4] vividly conveys Helen Kling's commitment to saving the barn as included below:

Helen Kling got to be almost ninety years old…long enough to see her most cherished dream come true—the end of a successful eighteen-year-long struggle to save an important part of her life. An old barn.

It wasn't just any old barn, although you could tell it was as tired as many old barns you see. Thing is, this one was round… This old round barn was built by pioneer farmer Samuel Laughlin in 1883…that was before Washington became a state…a century later in 1983, the barn needed help. Lots of help. Just how many more winds could it lean into without falling down?

Not long after, the Laughlins retired to the little family cemetery up the gentle slope of pasture behind the barn. Helen's own family took over the farm. That's where Helen grew up from baby to toddler to adult. And even though Helen Kling moved away…the ownership of the farm ultimately was hers. Anyone who got to know Helen also got to know the reason, she simply rented out instead of selling the old place. It was for love of the barn.

Helen's eyes got misty one day back in 1983 when she surveyed the decrepit, aged structure as it creaked and seemingly swayed in a sudden burst of wind. Her voice choked back a sob… "That old barn just can't fall down," she sighed.

Helen grew up here on the rural farm…Her earliest recollection was when, at the age of five, she climbed to the haymow to see a new litter of kittens. "It was easy enough climbing up there to the loft," she recalled. "But I couldn't get down, so I did what I did best. I bawled until someone rescued me." With memories like those, no wonder Helen Kling loved the old round barn so much.

But others loved it, too. That love was reflected in people's efforts that got it placed on the National Register of Historic Places. They formed a group called The Cowlitz Round Barn Preservation Association. Calls went out for volunteer labor, materials, and funding.

In 1995, blackberry brambles were still climbing the barn's walls, sunshine and rain were still streaming and leaking through its cracks and decay. More than ever, it was showing signs of its ancient age. It leaned so far that one wondered how it could still stand.

And then the thing Helen feared the most happened. Seventy-five miles-per-hour winds tore at the barn until it toppled. Collapsed. Gave up. But not Helen Kling (Figure II.2.5).

"I figured," she said, "if the barn was going to be preserved—resurrected, actually—I'd just have to do it myself." But as it turned out, she wasn't alone.

There was some timber on the old home place. She sold some of it for funding; some of the timber became lumber for rebuilding the barn. Old round barn T-shirts went on sale to further bolster the coffers. Donations of material and volunteer laborers, chief among them her renters Tony and Alex Selander, began to arrive.

The center pole went up, then the walls and the roof. People who thought the barn was a goner saw a new birth. So there, three years later, stood the brand new old round barn. Sturdy and brilliant in its bright new coat of paint. Red…

Figure II.2.5: The barn in 1980 before the destructive storm.

And now Helen Kling lies up there in the tiny cemetery, with a view between an archway of fir trees that perfectly frames the barn where, so long ago, a little girl climbed to the hayloft to see some newborn kittens (Figure II.2.6)

Figure II.2.6: Helen Kling's final resting place (along with the Laughlins) overlooking her beloved barn.

Thank you, Helen Kling, Tony and Alex Selander, and their friends from the Cowlitz Round Barn Preservation Association. Your collective dedication to rebuild and restore the barn will delight and enrich the lives of many for generations (Figure II.2.7)—hopefully, many will be motivated to save other barns and enhance our appreciation of the rural landscape and culture.

Two Mysteries

The State Survey form prepared by Michael Neuschwanger in 1985 alludes to two mysteries. First, Neuschwanger writes, "It is possible, but less likely, that the barn was built later, in the 1910s following contemporary interest in round barn design. This interest was spurred by an experiment on demonstration dairy farms conducted by the [University] of Illinois, in 1908… advanced this form on the basis of a lesser quantity of materials for a given volume. Many journals touted the advantages of round barn design." The reference continues to support the 1883 date stating that "if the barn was built in the 1910s, it would be contrary

Figure II.2.7: The restored barn with its T-extension in 2015.

to how sketchy family histories [are], which indicate that Laughlin built the barn and he died in 1910."[5] We also support the 1883 date.

The second mystery is implied in the following: "In either case, the barn is the last standing round barn in Cowlitz or Wahkiakum Counties. A much larger dairy barn in Wahkiakum County, which was clearly influenced by contemporary design of the 1910s, has fallen within the last two years." Was there another round barn? If so, we could not locate it. Perhaps Mr. Neuschwanger was referring to the tragic collapse of the round barn outside of Skamokawa in 1982. (Reference the Wiester Round Barn, pp. 71–75.)

On 22 February 2015, we headed for another surprise when we stopped to see the barn in Castle Rock. It was in bad shape when we had last visited in 1980 and we thought it would have collapsed. As we rounded the bend, we were delighted to discover it had been beautifully restored. We stopped to get permission to photograph it. As we walked to the house, two protective men came out: Tony and Alex Selander. We both thought, "oh dear, this might be a challenge." After our introductions, they turned out to be the kindest, most interesting caretakers of the barn. They explained they had moved to the property in 1986 and during their very first night there, a storm blew most of the roof away. Then, with the help of Helen Kling and the Cowlitz Round Barn Preservation Association, they started to rehabilitate the structure. They had abundant stories of how it was done, including the many ideas of finding alternative uses for the restored barn

and forming a working historic farm and museum (an ideal celebratory use of this amazing building). They also discussed some of the difficulties they encountered along the way. During the restoration, the Cowlitz County building department had stopped the work and required architectural/engineering drawings that complied with 1890 codes. (This was a daunting task, but they did find funds to hire an engineer to research and prepare the required documentation.) The owners had to mill full dimension lumber to replace the decaying existing members and managed to get the cedar shingles for the roof donated. What amazing men! We were delighted with our discoveries and gained renewed energy and commitment to continue documenting the life of this and other wonderful buildings. WOW, we had fun.

The Round Barns in Whitman County

Since the majority of the following round barns were constructed between 1901 and 1920, we have decided to group the remaining five Palouse round barns together. They were all constructed in Whitman County and are a rather unique cluster of five round barns. Spokane County has two round barns and all other counties in the state with round barns have only one. The creative relationship with the state's land-grant institution, now Washington State University (WSU), and the round barns of the Palouse is unknown but could have been an influential factor. WSU has a proud, extensive tradition in agricultural science and production at the Pullman campus located in Whitman County as well as in other counties throughout the state with WSU extension agents.

As discussed earlier, Colfax, the county seat of Whitman County, is the center of the Palouse region in eastern Washington, where five round barns were built. It has a poetic relationship with our first U.S. President, George Washington, and Fairfax VA, where the nation's first round barn was built.

The Palouse is a beautiful rural landscape, (Figures II-1 and II-2) encompassing virtually all of Whitman County, Washington and adjoining Latah County, Idaho. The rolling hills are the perfect backdrop for round barns and other structures. The forever changing patterns found on the Palouse are a constant delight to residents and photographic hobbyists and professionals. The rolling hills are often steep, requiring farmers to plow with the contours of the land, further accentuating and harmonizing with the natural forms of the landscape.

The Palouse landscape also has dramatic changes with various sunlight patterns. The grain waves with the wind have striking changes with the growth and color of various crops and the seasons—snow white in winter, spring green during the early growing season and golden in late summer just before harvesting the grain (Figures II.3–5).

The Palouse climate and soil are ideally suited for growing wheat, oats, barley, lentils and peas. In August, Pullman has a national lentil festival to celebrate the global importance of lentils. The festival draws thousands of people from throughout the region and across the nation. The festival is discussed and illustrated in Chapter IV (pp. 182).

As discussed and illustrated for the Manning Barn, all five Palouse round barns were adapted from the original planned usage by dairy cows to effectively accommodate horses to supply "horsepower" for plowing and harvesting the vast, rolling grain fields of the Palouse (Figure II-6). In the 1930s, after the Great Depression, the tractor was found to be far more effective than the teams of horses. One owner stated, "In 1935, they were still harvesting the wheat crop in the usual fashion with their team of fine draft horses. But that year was different: during the frequent breaks taken to rest their tired horses, they watched as the neighbors harvested without stopping, using a tractor. It was the last harvest in which they used the draft horses…and have ever since relied upon internal combustion engines for their motive power."[6] After the age of horses for "horsepower," the round barns of the Palouse tried dairy farming and housed a few riding horses for their families as the face of agricultural production was changed forever.

Figures II.1 and II.2: The picturesque rolling wheat fields of the Palouse. The image on the right was taken looking north from the top of Kamiak Butte (8 miles north of Pullman), in the distance Steptoe Butte, one of the highest point in Whitman County.

Figures II.3, II.4, and II.5: Winter white, spring green, and harvest gold on the Palouse. Photo series courtesy of Ken Carper, WSU architecture colleague, professor emeritus, and now photographer, kencarperphotos.com.

Figure II.6: Harvesting the wheat on the rolling hills of the Palouse with teams of "real horsepower." Note, in the center of the image, a gasoline-powered automobile—soon thereafter horse-powered harvesting was replaced by the tractor. Image courtesy of WSU Libraries' MASC.

3. Manning Round Barn, 1900–1953

The Manning Barn was the first circular barn built on the Palouse and had the only "wedding layer cake" style two-level design with a double roof in the state.

Original Location: Round Barn Hill, on Highway 195, approximately five miles north of Pullman, Whitman County, Washington.

Original use: Horse barn without a silo in the center

Current use: Razed and removed in the 1950s

Characteristics: Round with a double cone-shaped gable roof. It was 80 feet in diameter and originally designed to house workhorses on the lower level and a hayloft on the upper level.

The Manning Barn was the first known round barn on the Palouse and was built by Ben Manning in 1900–01 (Figure II.3.1). The Mannings must have been innovators as theirs was not only the first of the five round barns constructed in Whitman County, but they also adapted the promised efficiency of the round barn for dairy cows to his workhorses. In the age before tractors, extensive teams of horses were used for harvesting the wheat and legumes on the hilly Palouse landscape (Figure II.3.2). The Mannings crowned their double-tiered round barn with a solid copper weathervane in the shape of a horse, symbolizing the primary use of the structure.

In 1910, Mr. C.T. Krous bought the Manning farm and barn. His daughter, Verna Krous, (later Mrs. Eugene Harms) stated why Mr. Manning decided on a round barn: "Ben had a lot of horses—maybe 30 head sometimes—and figured he could save a lot of time forking out the hay if he had them standing in a circle with heads all towards the center." Verna Krous also remembers with great delight the use of the hayloft: "One of my most happy recollections is of a swing we had hung from the high cupola in the middle of the barn. The extremely long ropes made swinging a real adventure." Verna also recalls, "A rather amusing thing about the structure was the way some of the WSC [Washington State College, now WSU] frats used it when they were initiating pledges. A group of new student recruits would often be sent to look for a note 'located in the northeast corner of the building' that contained further instructions. But, since the building was round, endless searching failed to reveal any note, of course!"[7] This is reminiscent of the reason the Shakers built their Hancock round barn—to eliminate those dark corners where mysterious notes (and possibly evil spirits) could hide.

The Manning Barn sat prominently on a hill five miles northwest of Pullman towards Colfax on Highway 195. It was quite a landmark, as the hill became known as "Round Barn Hill." In 1947, the farm was sold to Dr. F.A. Bryant, who was in partnership with Glenn Harlow, and in 1953 it was decided to raze the barn. When asked why the barn was being razed, Mr. Harlow replied, "It was no use as a place to store machinery and I keep only a few cows. Furthermore, the building was becoming rotten in spots. We found many round nails in it, and some square ones, too, as we tore it down. It was certainly well put together. As replacements, I'll probably put up a machine storage shed and a small barn." (Figure II.3.3)

When anyone commented on the disappearance of the old landmark, Mr. Harlow replied, "Oh yes, many have spoken about it, and some suggested that maybe I ought to put up a signboard saying, 'this is where the old round barn stood,' or something like that. Well, at any rate, I sure did hate to tear it down!" (Figure II.3.4 and II.3.5).

And YES, some 60 years later we agree: we miss it dearly and the only memory of the barn is in its photographs, stories, and that the land itself is still called "Round Barn Hill." (Figures II.3.6 and II.3.7).

Figure II.3.1: Exterior of the Manning Barn. This undated historic photo shows Ben Manning and his family standing in the barn's doorway. Photo courtesy of Washington State University historic archives.

Figure II.3.2: Harvesting the wheat with real horse (or mule) power. Photo courtesy of Washington State University historic archives.

Figure II.3.3: The razing of the Mannings' round barn on Round Barn Hill in the 1950s. The view shows the south side of the Mannings' house between the framing of the barn and the unusual approach to deconstructing the barn from the bottom up. The remaining upper story must have been very unstable at that point.

Figures II.3.4 and II.3.5: Top: Aerial view of the historic Manning farm today minus the round barn. The 1900 round barn was located to the south of the large rectangular machinery shed seen in the photo. (Google Maps).
Bottom: Front view of the property today, clearly showing the house and machinery shed.

Figures II.3.6 and II.3.7: Above: The Manning barn on Highway 195, circa 1940, with a Studebaker automobile parked just off the roadway. Photograph by Huntoon Progress Commission Photographs, courtesy of Washington State Archives. Below: A modern-day view of the Manning barn site on Round Barn Hill (2021), taken by the authors from approximately the same location as the historic image.

4. Steinke Polygon Barn, 1915

The Steinke Barn was the first 12-sided polygon barn to be built on the Palouse and the first dodecagonal in the state to use reinforced concrete on the lower walls.

Location: Highway 23, 4.7 miles west of St. John, Whitman County, Washington

Original use: The dairy and horse barn has a central manger for hay and oats (not a silo for silage). Like all the barns on the Palouse, the horses supplied the "horsepower" to plow the fields and harvest the grain before tractors. Later, the barn was used for cattle.

Current use: First level and loft are open and used for storage.

Characteristics: The 12-sided, dodecagonal barn is 60 feet in diameter across its side (or 62 feet across at the corners) with a segmented, conical gable roof and unique flared eaves to keep rain away from the lower walls. The first-floor walls were reinforced concrete, the first of only four round barns in the state to use this type of wall construction. The polygon retains the functional advantages of a round barn while the straight, linear segments create a more economic and efficient construction. The barn does not have a central silo but features a unique rectangular feeding bin or manger on the ground floor. There is no central support extending to the roof, creating a uniquely beautiful, uninterrupted dome ceiling enclosure to the loft. A custom-crafted wood cupola creates a fitting crown to the dome and provides light and ventilation.

The Max Steinke Barn is the second oldest historic "round" barn located on the western edge of Whitman County and the picturesque Palouse region of eastern Washington (Figure II.4.1). The 345-acre Steinke farm is located along Cottonwood Creek, 4.7 miles from the town of St. John (Figure II.4.2). The barn has numerous innovations and is being restored and cared for by the Steinke and DeChenne families, while also having the honor of being listed in the National Register of Historic Places.

Theodore Steinke purchased the property in the early 1900s and farmed there for a number of years before he leased it to his son, Max, and his wife Ida (Falls). The farm's primary purpose was to grow wheat and some barley. Like all the early farms and barns on the Palouse, Steinke maintained twelve draft horses for supplying the "horsepower" for plowing and harvesting the grain.

Max was an innovator and in 1915 he started planning and building a new barn. He must have been influenced by the literature on the economy and efficiency of round barns. His design, selected size, layout, and diameter parallel the contemporary literature (Figures II.4.3 and II.4.4). As the first 12-sided barn in Whitman County, it undoubtedly influenced others with Steinke's innovation as the two Hall brothers and the Leonard barns were built with similar size and geometry several years later and discussed in the following segments.

Max hired a carpenter and enlisted his younger brother, Walter, to help build the 60-foot-diameter polygon barn.

Besides selecting the "round" form, some of the other innovations were the early use of reinforced concrete for the walls (the first of four in the state); using a polygon rather than a round shape, in order to use linear wood products effectively (Figures II.4.5 and

Figure II.4.1: Exterior view of the Steinke (DeChenne) barn today.

Figure II.4.2: Aerial view of the Steinke (DeChenne) farm and round barn. (Google Maps)

II.4.6); and recycling wood salvaged from an earlier barn. Max installed a manure trolley system incorporating a single track on the ceiling around the inside perimeter of the barn, to facilitate the removal of animal waste/manure (Figures II.4.7, II.4.8, and II.4.9). Additionally, the curved ribs were constructed of 1 x 10 planks nailed together to form the arched ribs of the loft ceiling and enclosing roof. In 1915, the cost of the barn was $1,700. Following an old tradition, local families gathered for a barn dance to christen what was, without a doubt, Max Steinke's masterpiece…musicians played from the top of the chop bin in the center of the loft as neighbors and lovers, (some,

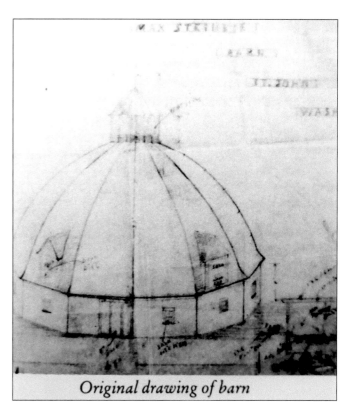

Original layout schematic of barn

Original drawing of barn

Figures II.4.3 and II.4.4: Historic plan and perspective drawing of the Steinke barn. Note in the plan the rectangular feeding bin and the twelve animal stalls relating to the twelve sides, each centered on the window or door openings. Originally, ten of the stalls housed two draft horses each (allowing room for twenty horses total), and the other two stalls housed three dairy cows each. These drawings, made by an unknown draftsman, are in the possession of Charles and Martha DeChenne

Figure II.4.5: The 12-segmented (dodecagon) roof construction and 16-foot diameter cupola providing light and ventilation.

undoubtedly, one and the same) danced about under the spacious dome.[8]

Then later in 1935, Max Steinke's daughter Martha and her husband, Charles DeChenne, moved to the farm. Upon visiting the farm in 2017, we were told that the Steinke and DeChenne families have a long-standing tradition to gather every summer from all parts of the country for a week to celebrate an enjoyable family reunion and to this day, continue work on restoring the barn. Thank you to the Steinke and DeChenne families for continuing to maintain this historic structure.

Max Steinke's barn "withstood the test of time and the elements. [His] structural masterpiece has outlasted nearly all other barns like it built in the region and continues to serve as one of the outstanding structural landmarks on the landscape of the Palouse." (Figures II.4.10 and Polygon II.4.11)[9]

Figure II.4.6: Interior view of the upper floor (used as a hayloft) and the beautiful unsupported dome and central cupola providing light and ventilation. Note the new vertical steel reinforcement of the twelve main ribs and steel horizontal cables or tension rings. The light roofing members are those replaced during the reroofing process.

Figures II.4.7, II.4.8, and II.4.9: Interior views of the barn's lower floor in 2016. In the left and right photos, note the overhead rail, which carried the manure trolley, and the gutter in the floor for easy cleaning. The historic photograph in the center shows the square central feeding manger as drawn in the original plan (Figure II.4.3). From Holstine, C. "Max Steinke Round Barn." Bunchgrass Historian, Whitman County Historical Society Quarterly, Fall 1989.

Figures II.4.10 and II.4.11: Above: Both the old and new segments of the roof are visable. Below: A perimeter steel cable (tension ring) and steel reinforcements to the 12 main ribs have been installed. The new cedar shingles and reinforcements were installed during the family's traditional summer gatherings.

Hall Brothers' Polygon Barns 1916–1980s

These two barns are the only "twin" barns in the state built by brothers on neighboring farms on the Palouse.

5. George Hall's Barn, 1916–1985

Original Location: Two miles west of Steptoe, north side of Highway 23, Whitman County, Washington.

6. Tom Hall's Barn, 1916–1979

Original Location: Three miles west of Steptoe, Highway 23, and approximately two miles south on old Green Hollow Road (now Blackwell Road), Whitman County, Washington.

Original uses: The barns were built for dairy cows and some horses. Most of the horses that were used to plow, plant and harvest their rolling fields were housed in a larger barn near Steptoe. At times, the horses numbered as many as 75. After the "horse" power shifted to the mechanical power of steam and later to gasoline/diesel combustion, the horses were no longer needed and the farm's use for horses diminished.

Current use: Neither barn currently exists

Characteristics: The barns were each a dodecagonal polygon, 60 feet in diameter with a conical, segmented, domed roof. The two-story barns were about 48 feet high, reaching another 12 feet to the top of the crowning cupolas (providing critically important ventilation). George Hall's barn had an imported metal cupola and Tom Hall had one built of wood by the contractor. Both barns had a central feeding area and clear-span roof framing creating uninterrupted dome ceilings and roofs. For sanitation, they had a Louden manure carrier attached to the upper floor beams to service the animals on the lower level.

George W. Hall emigrated from Tennessee to Steptoe, Washington, in 1901 at the age of 34, along with other families from Tennessee. In fact, Steptoe was called "Tennessee Flats" by many, and even had a street named Tennessee on which a school was built. The Hall brothers, George and Tom, built the pair of round barns in 1916 (Figures II.6.1 and II.6.9).[10] The barns were located approximately three miles apart on the brothers' separate but adjacent farms. Building twin round barns is unique in the state and it is unfortunate that both have disappeared from Whitman County and the picturesque Palouse landscape (Figures II.6.2, 3, 5, and 10). George Hall's full name was George Washington Hall. We wonder if the name related to the reason the Hall family moved to and homesteaded in Washington and built round barns—like the first known round barn in the United States, built by President George Washington in 1794 (Figure II.6.4).

Figures II.6.1 and II.6.2: Above, George Hall's farm and barn in 1975 and below, without the barn in 2010.

Both barns may have been influenced by Max Steinke and his barn just 18 miles to the west of the Hall brothers' farms. Like the Steinke barn, the Hall brothers used the polygon shape for more efficient construction. Both barns were constructed by the H.L. Weld Co. of Spokane. George Hall's house and barn cost $7,500, and his metal cupola was purchased for an additional $258 from Lincoln, Nebraska.[11] Both barns had concrete footings, floors and retaining walls to allow them to be built into hillsides, which allowed direct access to the upper-story haylofts for effectively unloading hay from horse-drawn carts. The circular pattern allowed the horse-drawn wagons to move through in a circular path without having to back up (Figures II.6–8).[12]

Unfortunately, the Tom Hall Barn collapsed due to a heavy wet snowstorm in 1979 (Figures II.6.9–11). George Hall's barn deflected but withstood the test of time until 1985 when it was finally pulled down by Norman Wilson, a grandson, using a cable and a powerful tractor—the stubborn beams of the dome, which had withstood many harsh winter storms, finally snapped by the huge mechanical forces of the tractor and the dome simply laid down (to rest). Ironically, like some humans, the remains were cremated, and the wood was disposed of in a controlled burn by the Steptoe fire department.[13]

Figure II.6.3: Aerial view of George Hall's farm in 2015 without the round barn. The barn's footprint shows as the circular shape in the upper right of the fenced farmyard. (Google Maps)

Figures II.6.4 and II.6.5: Left: Exterior of George Hall's barn in 1980 and right, the site without the barn in 2014. Note the shift in the dome caused by winter snow and windstorms (western winds coming from left to right) and possibly the heavy weight of the metal cupola.

Figures II.6.6, II.6.7, and II.6.8: Above, photo shows the dome above the second-floor hayloft of George Hall's barn. Below, photos show the lower level for the family's dairy cows and horses. Note the radial frame of the upper floor and central feeding area. The photo on the lower right is a mirrored image of the photo on the left. Figure II.6.6 has been photo enhanced by Rob Wagoner.

The George Hall barn was very photogenic as it stood along Highway 23 just off Highway 195, a much-traveled route between Pullman and Spokane. We often passed the barn during our travels. We watched and worried about its deflection and wondered if it would be restored by human energy or collapse due to natural forces. Nature won out: all that is left are fading memories and historic photographs.

We extended a final note of appreciation to the Hall family through the years for their help to us and the many students doing research projects on their beautiful barns. Mark Hall, a grandson of George W. Hall, still farms the Hall brothers' farms. In our most recent phone conversation with Mark, we expressed our sincere gratitude for his help, and he stated simply, yet profoundly, that "we believe in helping each other." Fortunately, we have found this philosophy to be true of most barn owners and we extend this same message to all, locally and globally.

Figure II.6.9: Tom Hall's barn before its collapse. Note the crowning wooden cupola. This black and white photo is courtesy of Connie Hall during our visit in 1980.

Figures II.6.10 and II.6.11: Left: The sad remains of Tom Hall's barn during our visit in 1980. The close-up image on the right reminds us of two sad eyes looking at us. (We had tears in our eyes, too.)

7. Leonard Polygon Barn, 1917

The Leonard Barn was the first known use of early laminated trusses from the nearby Potlatch Lumber Company.

Location: Old Moscow Highway, three miles west of Pullman, Whitman County, Washington

Original use: Dairy barn with a central silo for silage. Later, the barn was also used for horses to supply the "horsepower" to plow the fields and harvest the grain before tractors. Still later, the third floor was added in the second level loft for chicken and egg production.

Current use: Renewed and returned to its original spatial configuration. First level and loft are open and used for storage.

Characteristics: The dodecagonal barn is 60 feet in diameter with a conical segmented gable roof. Although the barn has a central silo, the silo doesn't extend and support the center of the roof—creating a unique, spacious, and uninterrupted dome ceiling and roof. It is 48 feet high to the top of the 12-segmented, domed roof and 62 feet high to the top of a new cupola, which is a fitting crown to the dome and provides for critically important ventilation. The original cupola blew off in a storm in the 1960s and was replaced in 2000-2001 along with major repairs that included shingling the roof and repainting the walls.

The Leonard Barn is a historic 12-sided "round" barn located in the picturesque Palouse region of eastern Washington and northern Idaho (Figure II.7.1). The round barn and rolling hills of the Palouse have a poetic harmony that are perfectly matched to each other via their organic forms. (Figure II.7.2).

The Leonard Barn was built in 1917 by its owner, Thomas Andrew Leonard. George Leonard, the son of Thomas Leonard, stated the barn was designed and constructed by his father with the help of Mr. Cline, a contractor and carpenter. The 60-foot dome was constructed by an early use of laminated trusses from the Potlatch Lumber Company, some 35 miles away in neighboring Idaho. George states that his father was influenced by some round barns in the state of Ohio. He also stated

that as a child, he remembers having a book of pictures and plans of barns, some of which were round barns. This book was thought to be a catalog by the Louden Machinery Company, based in Fairfield, Iowa. Leonard continues that his dad said he had built the barn round so that he could have the animals facing inward, to better feed them in the center and care for them from the perimeter daylight. For cleaning purposes, a carriage system allowed the manure to be removed while retaining a flat floor. Before the days of electricity, perimeter windows were installed to give light to the work zone.[14]

The above statements parallel the early scientific agricultural studies published by the University of Illinois (UI)—optimizing the production and cost of dairy production. As discussed earlier, these

landmark studies stated that the "round" barn forms were the most functionally efficient and cost-effective barn forms. There exists a close correlation between the dates of these agricultural publications and the actual size and layout of the Leonard barn. There may have been some influence and collaboration with the WSU Agricultural Department located just three miles to the east as WSU was familiar with those same UI studies about the more efficient 12-segmented construction design form. They could well have also influenced the Hall brothers in the construction of their barns some 35 miles north of WSU, as well as Max Steinke's barn some 50 miles northwest of the campus. Also, like the Steinke barn, Leonard used the unusual flared eaves to keep rainwater away from the

Figure II.7.1: Exterior view of the Leonard Barn today. It is a historic 12-sided "round" barn located in the picturesque Palouse region of eastern Washington and northern Idaho. The round barn and rolling hills of the Palouse have a poetic harmony, matched to each other via their organic forms.

Figure II.7.2: Aerial view of the Leonard Farm and round barn. (Google Maps)

lower walls. Unlike the Hall and Steinke Barns, Leonard used wooden construction throughout instead of concrete for the first level walls, and he put three windows for increased light in the lower wall segments instead of one used by the other barns.

The Leonard Barn has adapted to many changes in farming practices down through the years, from a dairy barn to housing horses when the surrounding wheat fields were harvested by real horsepower and then, a third level was built in the loft for a large poultry and egg

production facility. The third level has since been removed, exposing the beautiful radial structure of its dome roof (Figures II.7.3–5). Externally, the barn remains in its original 12-sided round form.

The Leonard family has been instrumental in maintaining their family barn. In the 1970s, George Leonard, at the age of 80, re-shingled major parts of the roof and repainted the exterior walls with the original green color (Figures II.7.6 and II.7.7). He received a State Historic Preservation award for his work. In 2000–2001, the family established a barn restoration fund, solicited community support along with considerable family resources and received a state grant to replace the important crowning cupola, which had blown off many years earlier, and made substantial repairs to the dome caused by water damage. They

Figures II.7.3, II.7.4 and II.7.5: Top: Interior view of the upper floor (hayloft), central silo, and beautiful dome roof of the Leonard Barn. The framing shows the repairs made in 2000–2001 when the rain cap-cupola was replaced. Bottom: Interior views of the lower floor of the barn in 2016. The image on the right is the original photograph, the one on the left is a mirrored view to show the full extent of the lower circular floor with the silo in the middle.

also repaired the windows and repainted the barn to its original color. At a "barn reopening celebration," they had 1500 guests who signed into the guest book. It was a major restoration effort to save this wonderful barn for future generations interested in the state and country's rural culture heritage, landscape and early architectural advancements.

Because of the Leonard Barn location, just three miles from the authors' Pullman home, it is one of our favorites. We often took visitors and students to see this well-maintained barn and George Leonard was always gracious in allowing us to visit and explore the barn. It motivated our interest in searching out the various round barns in the state.

Tom, along with other colleagues, used the barn for student design projects in historic preservation and adaptive reuse (Figure II.7.8). It was a joint collaborative studio with the landscape architecture department. The student teams generated a broad variety of unique project designs for its use including an outdoor historic museum to agriculture, a nursery and gardens, a farmer's market, and even a garden restaurant specializing in the foods produced on the Palouse.

In the mid-1970s, Tom and Jerry Young were asked to give a presentation to the State Historic Society on their research into the round barns and silos of Washington. Jerry was interested in silos and, of course, Tom was intrigued with round barns. They titled the presentation, "Round Forms and Rural Ruins of Washington." When we presented the Leonard Barn, we mentioned George Leonard's kindness, pride, and dedication in maintaining his family's barn and, at the age of 80, he was reshingling the roof and planned on repainting the walls the original green color, which the family accomplished in 2001. After the talk, they voted to give him a State Historic Preservation Award. The next time we met, George asked Tom if he was the one who "caused all the fuss" about the barn. Tom thought, "Oh dear, what happened?" Then with a smile, George expressed how delighted he was to get the award. It was definitely one of those special "round barn moments" in our lives.

As illustrated in their architectural drawings (Figures 11.7.9-11), WSU architecture students Steve Nys and David Burger developed a Historic American Buildings Survey of the barn for the Library of Congress (HABS No. WA-168).[15] The Leonard Barn received National Historic Registration and in 1986, Nys and Burger received the National Peterson Award—a coveted award for the best historic building submissions of the year. The drawings included here are only three of the ten drawings developed by the WSU students for the Historic Buildings Survey.

The last time Tom visited the barn was in September 2016. He wanted to just stop in and see if it was still standing tall on the Palouse. Much to his surprise and delight, the Leonard family was there and had cleaned the barn and set up a special display of the barn's history, including its awards and family history. They were preparing for a group of visitors from the Idaho State Historical Society. The Leonard family was so gracious in reviewing the exhibition and family albums with Tom and allowing him to update our photo collection. Yes, the Leonards and their barn are really special. (Figure II.7.12)

In 2016, with Tom's encouragement, the Leonard Barn was selected as one of the 100 most important buildings in Washington for Archipedia, a program developed by the National Society of Architectural Historians to celebrate the significant works of architecture in each state (https://sah-archipedia. org/). Tom was asked to write a summary and it can be reviewed at the SAH Archipedia website.[16]

Figures II.7.6 and II.7.7: George Leonard's efforts in re-shingling the family barn, 2001.

Figure II.7.8: WSU architecture students studying the barn for their assigned design project in 1991.

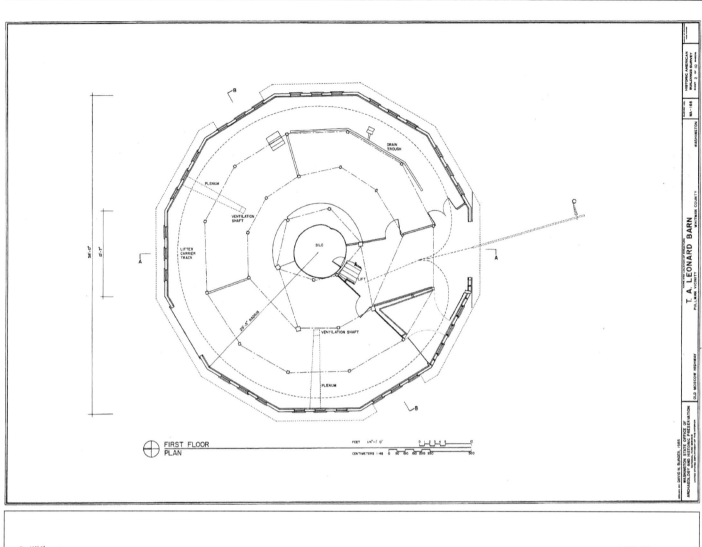

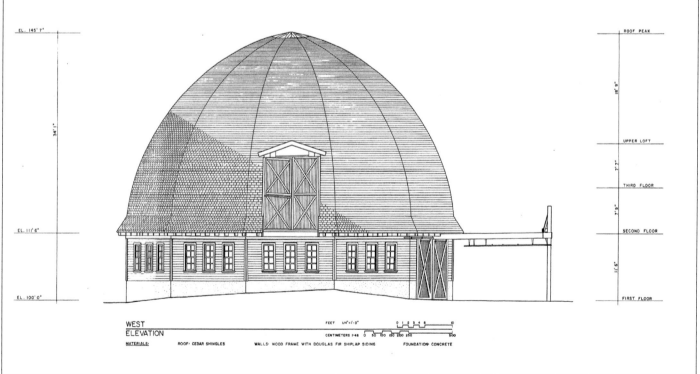

Figures II.7.9 and II.7.10: The drawings of the barn's plan (top) and elevation (bottom) of the 1985 Building Survey.

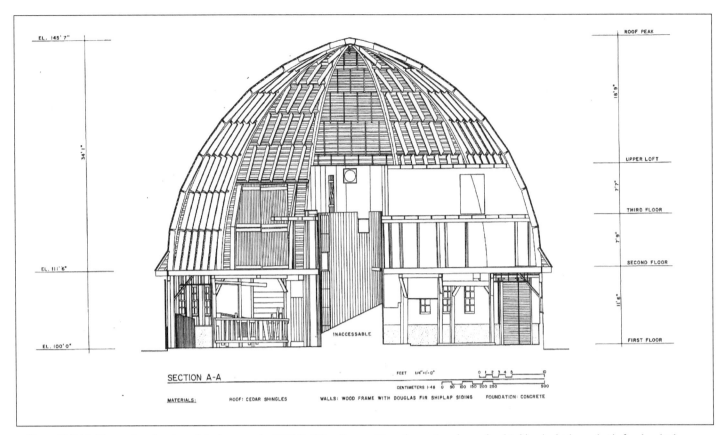

EL. 145'7"

34'1"

ROOF PEAK

18'9"

UPPER LOFT

7'2"

THIRD FLOOR

7'9"

SECOND FLOOR

EL. 111'6"

11'6"

EL. 100'0"

FIRST FLOOR

INACCESSABLE

SECTION A-A

FEET 1/4"=1'-0"   0 1 2 3 4 5   10

CENTIMETERS 1:48   0 50 100 150 200 250   500

MATERIALS: ROOF: CEDAR SHINGLES   WALLS: WOOD FRAME WITH DOUGLAS FIR SHIPLAP SIDING   FOUNDATION: CONCRETE

Figure II.7.11: The section drawing of the barn on the 1985 Building Survey. Note the section shows the third level which was built for the chickens. This level was removed subsequently by the Leonard family, exposing the beauty of the dome.

Figure II.7.12: The Leonard Barn is so beloved and notable in Pullman that a bas-relief of it was etched into an exterior brick wall of the Neill Public Library in Pullman.

8. Coffman Round Barn and Carriage House, 1902

This is the only known circular round barn built for agricultural purposes but specifically designed to fit into a unique residential location.

Location: 637 NW St. Helens Ave, Chehalis, Lewis County, Washington

Original use: Dairy barn with a silo in the center and carriage house.

Current use: Storage and garage.

Characteristics: The Coffman round barn has three stories with a central silo. It is 60 feet in diameter with a conical shaped (gable) roof and a unique central cupola for ventilation. It has a unique T-shaped addition at the front with classical characteristics and proportions to gracefully fit it to the surrounding residential neighborhood. It was originally designed as a carriage house for horses on the mid-level, a dairy barn on the lower level and a hayloft around the silo on the third mezzanine level. It is the only three-level barn in the state of Washington. Its location is unique as well, as it is in a residential area of Chehalis.

Mr. Noah B. Coffman and his wife moved to Chehalis in 1883. Coffman established an insurance, real estate and law practice office, and eventually opened the Coffman, Dobson & Co. bank. Along with his associates, he was instrumental in the early development of Chehalis.[17]

Mr. Coffman and his son had a personal interest in dairy farming and built up a Jersey herd, finally building this family barn in about 1902. The innovative barn had three levels, which were useful for family carriages and horses at the street level with a dairy barn below relating to the farming portion of the land (Figures II.8.1 and II.8.2). The barn also has a partial hayloft mezzanine to feed the horses and dairy herd along with the silo in the center (Figures II.8.3–5). Special care was taken to design a barn to fit the character of the residential street. The carriage house level (now used as a garage) has a perfectly proportioned classical portal (See Figure II.8.1) and side wings to fit in the residential character of the neighborhood. The round form allowed the carriages to circle around without having to back out. Today the location afforded another unique honor to the barn; it is the only barn in Washington listed as part of a National Register Historic District.

Mr. Coffman was concerned about sanitation. The cupola (Figure II.8.6) provided excellent ventilation and the barn was cleaned regularly. The manure was used to enrich the adjacent farm fields on the lower level.[18] (Figure II.8.7)

Because the Coffman barn is so unusual, we have visited it many times when traveling through the area. It is readily accessible because it was in a residential area close to the Chehalis city center. As such, it was one of our favorite destinations when we had friends and visitors with us. On our last visit in 2018, we observed the barn had a good roof and ventilation but did notice the round siding boards had some wear.

Figure II.8.1: Street-level view of the Coffman round barn in 2017. The residence is to the left of the driveway.

Figure II.8.2: Aerial view of the Coffman round barn and surrounding residential neighborhood. Note that the unique three-level barn serves as a carriage house on the residential level and as a dairy barn on the lower level, with pasture and agriculture land to the south and southwest. (Google Maps)

Figures II.8.3, II.8.4, and II.8.5: Top: Composite photograph of levels 2 (carriage house) and 3 (mezzanine hayloft) showing the beautiful dome framing and supportive silo in the center. Bottom: Ground floor (dairy level) where the cows would stand for milking and feeding around the central silo.

Figure II.8.6: The beautiful cupola crowning the conical roof providing critical ventilation. On the very top is a house for the neighborhood birds and a weather vane that also serves as a lightning rod. The small gable windows in the roof provide daylight to the upper levels.

Figure II.8.7: The Coffman Barn as seen from the lower level, showing the former pasture and farming land to the right (now a neighborhood park). The landscape and walkway are designed to accent the barn.

9. and 10. Seitz/Frazier Polygon Barns, 1903

This pair of octagonal barns is one of the most innovative in the state. The smaller octagon was built over a deep well with a cistern on the upper level that provided gravity-fed fresh water to the nearby home.

Location: 3991 Powerline Road, Walla Walla, Walla Walla County, Washington

Original use: Main structure was a working horse barn with some dairy cows. There is also an adjacent smaller barn located over a water cistern, which was used as a milk barn and blacksmith shop.

Current use: Equipment and storage

Characteristics: The two barns have a stunning setting and unique geometric roof forms. Both are eight-sided octagons. The larger barn is 56 feet in diameter and the smaller one is twenty-five feet across with two large, segmented extensions. The beautifully segmented roofs accent the octagon plans. The larger barn also has two gable roof extensions for loading hay into the second-floor loft and both have unique crowning cupolas. The Frazier Trust, the current owner, has replaced the shingles with a good asphalt shingle roof—a most important improvement to maintain the integrity of the structure.

The James Seitz family moved to Walla Walla in 1886 and started to build the barns in approximately 1903 (Figures II.9.1 and II.9.2) The larger octagonal barn was for working horses to plow the fields and harvest the grain (much like the barns built in the Palouse Region in adjacent Whitman County). The Seitz family also had a small herd of dairy cattle housed in the barn. The smaller octagonal barn was built about the same time as the larger barn for a blacksmith shop.

The Seitz family members were progressive innovators, as their round barns were the third earliest in Washington state. Seitz drew the plans (Figure II.9.3), cut the lumber and built both structures (Figures II.9.4–9). It proved more effective to build the straight eight walls and segmented roof with conventional, linear-sized lumber.

Mr. Seitz's blacksmith shop in the smaller octagon barn has a cistern in the upper story, high enough to supply gravity-fed fresh water to the house. He had a large engine, which powered his machinery (drill press, forge, etc.) and generated electricity as well. Mr. Seitz also designed the unusual windows that slide into the wall framing to create a full opening instead of only sliding halfway like the windows commonly used today (Figures II.9.10 and II.9.11).

Besides the barns, the Seitz family residence was, as stated in the Heritage Barn Register[19] as "modern as a city home and is a monument to the enterprise and progressive spirit of the owner. Everything about [their] place is kept in good repair and fences divide the farm into fields of convenient size, so that the work is carried on more advantageously. He utilizes the latest improved machinery to facilitate the work of plowing, planting and harvesting, and in wheat production, he displays most progressive methods in handling the crop, which is a very large one, as the soil is excellently adapted for the production of that cereal. He is also successfully engaged in stock raising. He is a man

Figure II.9.1: The Seitz/Frazier barns' unique roof geometry is set against the beautiful background of the foothills of the Blue Mountains.

Figure II.9.2: Above: Aerial view of the two Seitz (now Frazier) barns. (Google Maps)

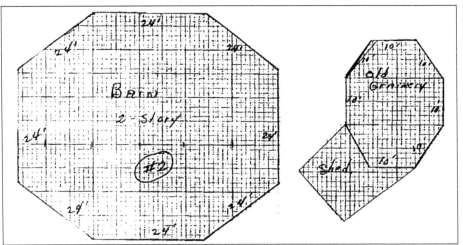

Figure II.9.3: Original plans of the two octagon barns, sketched by Mr. Seitz prior to beginning construction in 1903. The grid paper surrounding the plans was removed to accent the shape of the buildings.

of pronounced business ability in his chosen line of endeavor and is constantly seeking out new methods which will promote his interests and augment the productiveness and the general value of his farm."[20]

These barns were two of the last barns we "discovered" in the state of Washington, after a WSU architecture student told us of their existence. We tried to visit the barns in 2016, but their foreman would not allow entry without permission from the owner, Mr. Frazier, nor would he give us a contact number. We obtained a home address for the Fraziers while we were in Walla Walla. but, as it was located in a gated community, we were only able to leave a message and hoped they would contact us in return. Fortunately, Mr. Frazier returned our call and was willing to show us the barns the next time we were in Walla Walla. In 2018, we arranged a visit and Mr. Frazier was most gracious in showing us the two barns, discussing recently reroofing them both as well as his plans for ongoing restoration.[21]

The Frazier family also has a family museum in Milton-Freewater, Oregon, seven miles south of Walla Walla. This adventure reinforces our strong recommendation to always get prior permission to visit any of the barns.

Figures II.9.4, II.9.5, II.9.6, II.9.7, and II.9.8: Top: Composite photographs of the interior of the upper story of the barn—left, center and right (a mirrored image of the left photograph). Bottom: Photos of the ground level (the right is the mirrored image of the left).

Figure II.9.9: View of the small barn with its 16-foot extension. The larger barn is in the background. The people in the photo show the huge scale of the two barns.

On our second visit, we had a surprise, once again serendipitously tied to Pullman and to WSU where we lived for forty years. We noticed a new building just before the entrance to the Frazier property with the name "DOUBLEBACK." It was not open yet, but we did know of the Doubleback wines produced in Walla Walla. After our tour of the barns, we asked Mr. Frazier about the Doubleback building and he stated it was being built as a winery by Drew Bledsoe (Figure II.9.12). Being from WSU, Drew was renowned as an outstanding quarterback on the Cougar football team in the early 1990s. He led the team into one of national ranking. One of our most memorable games was the win in the Apple Cup with the University of Washington during a blizzard. The game is legendary and is often referred to as the "Snow Bowl." Drew holds many WSU and Pac-10 conference records and was named the Pac-10 offensive player of the year in 1992. He was drafted by the New England Patriots as the number one pick in the 1993 National Football League (NFL) draft. He had 14 outstanding years in the NFL, breaking numerous records and leading his team to two Super Bowls. He now focuses his time creating quality wines, participating in many philanthropic organizations, volunteering as a high school coach and as a sports commentator.[22] This makes a fun, yet surprising, connection between these two round barns, WSU, and our home in Pullman.

Figures II.9.10 and II.9.11: Left image is of the exterior of sliding windows, waiting to be restored. Right image is of the ground-level interior, showing coffee cans used as hangers.

Figure II.9.12: The Doubleback winery with the two Frazier round barns in the distant right.

11. Duskin Round Barn, 1916–1997

This barn is the only circular round barn in the northwest region of the state known to have a large, rectangular extension.

Location: Arlington, Snohomish County, Washington

Original use: Dairy barn with a hayloft on the second floor

Current use: Demolished in approximately 1997

Characteristics: The barn had a circular plan without a silo in the center. It had a large T-shaped rectangular segment. The round segment was 53 feet in diameter with a cone-shaped gable roof and copula and was 48 feet tall (52 feet to the top of the crowning cupola). It had cedar shingles enhancing the curved and rectangular walls, with two silos attached to the round segment on the south side. It is thought that the round portion was constructed first, prior to building the rectangular part of the barn.

◆

The Duskin Barn was built by Joe and Ruby Duskin in 1916 and was the only known round barn in the northwest region of the state (Figure II.11.1). It was particularly unique as this area was known for dairy farming.

The land, commonly referred to as the Kent Prairie, was originally owned by George Murphy who had a cattle farm and meat processing plant in Arlington.

Joe Duskin lived in Seattle and came to Arlington to work for Mr. Murphy.

Later, the Duskins purchased their land for a dairy farm, built the house in 1914, and completed the barn two years later (Figure II.11.2) They established The Maple Nook Dairy—successfully producing and delivering

Figure II.11.1: The Duskin farm and barn in 1986

Figure II.11.2: Aerial view of the farm and barn. Note the two silos on the far (south) side of the circular section.

their dairy products throughout the community of Arlington and adjacent areas. Unfortunately, in 1931 Mr. Duskin fell off the silo and was killed.

Figure II.11.3: The round segment of the Duskin barn with a milk house on the left, 1986.

The dairy enterprise was then continued by the family.[23] (Figure II.11.3)

The farm was sold to Penny Clark and later to a developer for a residential subdivision development. It is unfortunate that the barn was torn down in 1997 and the original and more stable round segment could not have been saved as it was inherently the more stable of the two portions of the structure (Figure II.11.4–8).[24]

We were tempted to call the Duskin Barn "the Arlington mystery barn." We always thought there should be some round barns in the northwest region of Washington as it was a dairy producing area. In the mid-1980s, a WSU architecture student told us about this barn in Arlington and we visited it in 1986, taking many of the barn photographs included here. We had a nice chat with the owner at the time and she kindly showed us the construction drawing (Figure II.11.9) and the aerial photographs (Figures II.11.11 and II.11.12). It was one of the last barns we discovered.

In 2016, we started to update our research and tried to relocate the barn to obtain current information and take additional photographs of this beautiful structure. In 1986, it had a good roof and seemed to be in excellent condition. We looked forward to seeing it again. We thought we knew the location and spent many hours "flying" over the Marysville-Arlington corridor via Google maps, searching for it without success.

To unlock the mystery, we called a number of people who are involved in the history of the area. Tom spoke with Ken Cage, president of the Marysville Historical Society, who kindly agreed to ask his colleagues about the barn, but no information was found. We then called the WSU agricultural extension service with, again, no leads. The kind Mount Vernon extension agent even sent out a request for information and

photos to his contact list of farmers in the county. No one responded. Finally, we called the *Marysville Globe and Arlington Times* newspaper and spoke with Steve Powell, the editor. He recommended sending a Letter to the Editor that included photographs of the barn. We followed his recommendation (Figure II.11.13) but, again, had no immediate responses. We thought it must have disappeared from the location and/or our memories had failed. Disappointed, we started to document the barn as a "mystery Arlington barn" in hopes that potential readers would add to our information base sometime in the future.

Then, we had three sequential and amazingly serendipitous surprises. The first happened at a gathering of past WSU colleagues, alumni, and friends in Seattle. A young man came up to us and asked if Tom was a past WSU architecture educator. Tom, of course, said, yes, he was. The young man told us he was an alumnus of the architecture program and remembered us. Then, out of the blue, he mentioned our interest in round barns and rural structures, and reported that a fellow student had done a report on the Arlington barn. What an amazing coincidence and potential connection. He stated he would try to contact this former student, and with his help, we finally talked to his contact. Unfortunately, the former student did not have a copy of his report, but he recommended calling Dale Duskin, one of the three sons of the family who built the barn. In a happy coincidence, the next day Dale Duskin called us, in response to the letter to the editor we had published. He was delighted to see the photos we had of his family's barn. Sadly, he confirmed that the barn no longer existed. His family had sold the farm to a developer and while it had been agreed that the barn would

Figure II.11.4: The barn with its T-extension, 1986.

Figure II.11.5: The intersection of the rectangular and radiating framing, beautifully accented by light from the crowning cupola. Photographed in 1986.

be saved for possible future use as a community center, it was torn down in 1997. The developer had stated that the rectangular segment had become unstable and a safety hazard, despite the promise to maintain it and find an alternative use for it. We hope that at least the lumber from it was recycled and reused in other structures (possibly in the new homes built on the property).

Lastly, the next day we got an email from Ken Cage at the Marysville Historical Society, stating that there was indeed a round barn in Arlington and we should contact Dale Duskin. The probability of all these connections happening within just a few days of each other was truly amazing. We feel so grateful to have been able to interview Dale Duskin and document this lost structure. Dale also developed a website for all the information and photographs.

Figures II.11.6, II.11.7, and II.11.8: Top: The interior of the second-level hayloft and beautiful clear span dome roof in 1986. Note the rail and hay lift used to distribute the hay throughout the round and rectangular segment of the structure. Bottom: The interior of the round segment's ground floor in 1986. The photograph on the left is a mirrored image of the one on the right.

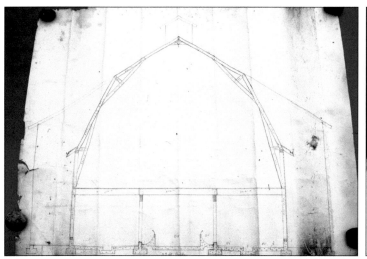

Figures II.11.9 and II.11.10: On the left, an early engineering section of the rectangular segment of the barn. Note the round segment is shown in background and the existing roof was built as a straight gable to match the round segment (not a segmented gambrel roof as drawn). The photo on the right shows a family goat watching over our activities.

Figures II.11.11 and II.11.12: Aerial views of the Duskin farm: on the left, in 1992, showing the barn, and on the right, in 2015, the subdivision without the barn. (Google Maps)

Letter to the Editor:

I am searching for information about a unique round barn in the Arlington-Marysville area. I photographed it in 1986 and would appreciate learning more about its specific location and history. If you have any information contact me at 206.780.5589 or tbartuska@ arch.wsu.edu.

Tom Bartuska, Bainbridge Island

Figure II.11.13: A clipping of the "Letter to the Editor" that Tom sent to *The Arlington Times/The Marysville Globe*, along with a photo of the barn. Note that the email address listed has changed to: tbartuska@wsu.edu

12. Wiester Round Barn, 1914–1981

The Wiester Barn had a conical domed roof with a matching cupola crown—the only one of its kind in the state—as well as a large, rectangular extension.

Location: Five miles north of Skamokawa on the east side of Middle Valley Road, Wahkiakum County, Washington

Original use: The barn was built for a rather large dairy farm

Current use: The barn no longer exists

Characteristics: The barn was a 60-foot diameter, two-story circular structure with a long rectangular T-shaped addition. The rectangular addition appears to have been added later as the dairy farm expanded. It was built on the hillside, so the upper level had easy access to store hay to feed the cows below. Like all round barns, the horse-drawn hay wagons could make a circle without having to back up out of the loft.

◆

The Howard Wiester family built their barn in 1914 for a large dairy farm with the assistance of contractor Clarence Winters.[25] (Figure II.12.1) The Skamokawa (pronounced "ska-mock-a-way") Valley has an ideal climate and soil composition for dairy farm production. The transition to farming from its logging and fishing past was helped by the state's first agricultural extension agent, George Nelsen (likely from Washington Agricultural College and School of Science, now Washington State University). The success of the earlier Nutter round barn (built in 1872, seven miles northwest of this barn) and George Nelsen, who helped promote awareness of the productivity and efficiency of round barns, may have influenced the Wiester family to consider building a round barn.

George Nelsen expressed that, as many farmers subscribed to the fund to support the county agricultural agent, they were anxious "…to have me visit their farms to assist them with such problems as planning crops for next year, planning barns and silos, reorganizing farms, teaching agriculture in the public schools, etc."[26]

Unfortunately, in the winter of 1981–82, wind and a heavy, wet snowstorm collapsed the barn and its T-shape extension (Figure II.12.2). The aging and missing shingles (the "starlight" quality of the interior dome) (Figure II.12.5) are a sign of potential water damage to the structure. Although the round form is significantly stronger than a rectangle form, wind and heavy, wet snow was more than it could withstand in its damaged condition. It was estimated to have had 150,000 wood shingles, so we understand the enormous challenge to re-shingling such a large dome. One source states that the barn collapsed in 1983, but we have photographs of the site without the barn dated in 1982.[27]

The town has a rather poetic name: it is named after a friendly native—Skamokawa, meaning *smoke of fog on the water*.[28] The county's name,

Wahkiakum, was also the name of the tribe that shared this area with the early settlers. Lewis and Clark stopped and received help from the Wahkiakum tribe,[29] where these names are so special to this charming town along the Columbia River. Irene Martin, in her delightful book on the area states:

> *A family of tourists was driving along Ocean Beach Highway on the lower Columbia and stopped for gas at a service station.*
>
> *"Say, what town is this?" asked the driver.*
>
> *"Cathlamet," answered the attendant.*
>
> *"What county are we in?"*
> *"Wahkiakum."*
>
> *"What's the next town?"*
> *"Skamokawa."*
>
> *The man turned to his wife. "Let's get out of here. No one seems to speak English."*[30]

With the rich dairy production in Skamokawa, a co-operative cream-

Figure II.12.1: The Howard Wiester farm and barn in 1980, showing the long T-shape extension. See Figure II.12.2 (below), taken from the same location in 1982, after the barn had collapsed in a storm.

Figure II.12.2: The rural ruins of the collapsed Wiester barn in 1982.

Figures II.12.3 and II.12.4: Above: Aerial view of the Howard Wiester farm (now owned by the Gribskobs), minus its formerly magnificent round barn. The round barn footprint is approximately just to the left of the 100-ft. scale symbol. The original T-extension, although it was much larger, is where the brown roof of the building (currently used as an artist's studio) is located. [Google Maps]. Below: The exterior of the Wiester barn in 1980.

ery was developed and specialized in producing butter. Their butter kept winning state and regional awards and helped the local farmers to prosper. So, who knows?…maybe the round barn helped to enrich the local dairy products.[31]

The current owners of the Wiester family farm are the Gribskobs. Mr. Gribskob is a talented stained-glass artist and built the rectangular studio where the T-shaped segment of the barn had been constructed a century earlier (Figure II.12.3).

In the footnotes, we referenced a great deal of the above information from Irene Martin's delightful book on Skamokawa, *Skamokawa: Sad Years, Glad Years*. The cover of her book features a photograph taken by Steve McClain of the Wiester family round barn capped in snow.

In 1980, an architecture student told Tom about this barn. Fortunately, that year we were able to visit and photograph it, complete with its unique

Figures II.12.3, II.12.4, II.12.5, and II.12.6: The exterior and interior of the Wiester Barn (1980). Top: Note the unique dome roof as well as the 'star-like' feature of the interior when looking up into the dome. Unfortunately, that 'starlight appearance' shows where there were defective shingles and holes where they were missing, which allowed rainwater and snow melt to decay the roof beams and sheathing. That is what eventually caused the roof to weaken and finally collapse. Bottom: The lower level for family dairy cows (and probably horses) with a concrete silo in the center. The photo on the right is a mirrored image of the original photo on the left.

cupola, before it collapsed (Figures II.12.5–8). In 1982, we revisited the site and took photographs of its sad remains (Figures II.12.2 and II.12.9). It was tragic to see this magnificent barn disappear from its picturesque rural landscape—more rural ruins.

On our third visit in 2014, we had a rather disappointing day. On a lovely, sunny day while we were visiting Long Beach, Washington, we decided to take a return trip to Skamokawa and Cathlamet (about an hour's drive away) to check out and photograph both the Nutter Barn and the Wiester farm site. When we got to the Cathlamet barn, much to our dismay, we realized we had left our camera in Long Beach. We did make some good contacts while there, fortunately, but it was with disappointment that we returned to Long Beach that day, having not been able to take any photographs.

That evening, we decided to give it a second try on our way home. and we had an amazing time—proof that persistence pays. When we returned to the Skamokawa site and stopped along the road for some distant photographic views, a friendly man stopped to ask if we were having car problems or needed any help. We explained our interest and amazingly, he lit up—he knew the family and gave out tons of information about the history of the barn. It was another really delightful round barn experience. Later, we were able to talk to Irene Martin and purchase a copy of her book on the history of this little town and the barn. The Wiester family round barn was one of our favorites. Unfortunately, it has become a lost part of the vanishing rural landscape. But we are grateful we were able to take photographs of such a unique barn—both before and after it collapsed—to share and contribute to the historical record.

Figures II.12.8 and II.12.9: Above, the beautiful cupola, and below, its rural ruins after the collapse.

13. Cornell/Marble Ranch Round Barn, 1916

The Marble Ranch Barn is the state's most unusual barn with its circular form, "eye lid" windows and silo extending 25 feet above the conical gambrel roof.

Location: Pleasant and Prosser Road, Grandview, Yakima County, Washington

Original use: Dairy barn with a silo in the center

Current use: Storage

Characteristics: A true round barn with a central silo that extends through the conical two-segment, gambrel roof. The barn is 64 feet in diameter (an even 200 feet in circumference), and the silo is 16 feet in diameter (50 feet around). Besides the extended central silo, the barn has two other unique qualities. The first is the sculptural roof, which forms the small but graceful "eye lid" windows. The second is the beautiful internal bracing from the supportive silo to the roof framing. The barn was originally designed as a dairy barn on the lower level for cows facing around the central silo with a large hayloft on the upper level.

The Marble Ranch round barn was built between 1912 and 1916 for S.D. Cornell's dairy farm. It is one the state's most unusual barns with its pure round form, "eye lid" windows and silo extending 25 feet above the conical gambrel roof (Figure II.13.1). Later when the farm was sold to the Marble family, they proudly painted "Marble Ranch" on the extended silo as seen in Figure II.13.1. The homestead, historic house and barn are currently owned by the Sorensen Family and are listed on the National Register of Historic Places (Figure II.13.2).

In addition to the external features, the interior also has some special characteristics: a wood floor for the dairy cows all facing inward in milking stanchions for efficient feeding around the silo, and perimeter windows to allow for excellent daylight when milking the cows. The second level framing features radiating floor beams supported by the exterior wall, an inner circle, and a central silo. The second level (hayloft) has radial roof framing, crowned by an elaborate connection to the silo, earning it a unique status in the state of Washington (Figures II.13.3–5).

We have visited the Marble Ranch barn numerous times over the years. It is an iconic structure in the Grandview, Yakima County area of central Washington. In 1972, Tom was invited to fly to western Washington in his client's private plane for some consultation work. During the flight, the pilot mentioned they were near Grandview. Tom asked if they could fly over the Marble Ranch barn; it proved to be an exceptional experience circling this round barn that day (Figure II.13.6).

On our earlier visits, we had not been able to get permission to see and photograph the interior. Fortunately, in 2018 we called the current owner, Mr. Sorensen, and he kindly gave permission for us to see the extraordinary interior structure. We asked him if he had any future plans for the barn; he said he thought it would make a great winery. We agreed, although the crops grown around the barn now are extensively hops (Figure II.13.7 and II.13.8)—possibly a microbrewery set in the hops fields would be a perfect use.

Figure II.13.1: The Cornell Marble Ranch round barn. Note the sculptured eye-lid upper window.

Figure II.13.2: Aerial view of the Cornell Marble Ranch round barn and homestead. (Google Maps)

Figures II.13.3, II.13.4, and II.13.5: Top image: The beautiful crowning connection from the silo to the roof rafters. Middle image: The second level used for hay and silage. This image is a composite photo—the left half is the original and the right half is a mirrored image. They are merged together to show the grandeur of the upper loft, roof structure, and framework. Bottom image: The ground level for the dairy cows. Note the central silo, wood floor with recession gutter for cleaning, and excellent daylight for milking the cows.

Figure II.13.6: Aerial photograph of barn and homestead (1972). Note that the irrigation channel no longer exists.

Figure II.13.7: The Marble Ranch barn set within the hops fields.

Figure II.13.8: Mature hops fields in the Grandview area. Adobe free photo.

14. Minnehaha/Ayers/McGraph Polygon Barn, 1915

The geometry of this barn is unique in the state as the only decagon (10-sided barn) with a segmented clear span hayloft and no central support.

Location: 16751 Cottonwood Canyon Road, 13 miles west of Yakima, Yakima County, Washington

Original use: Dairy and cattle barn without a silo in the center

Current use: Farm equipment and storage

Characteristics: The barn is a 10-sided decagon with a beautifully crafted, segmented cone-shaped gable roof with a crowning cupola for light and ventilation. It is 50 feet in diameter from one side to the opposite side, or 52 feet from one corner across to the opposite corner. Originally, the barn was designed for dairy cows and cattle on the lower level and a huge 24-foot-high hayloft on the second level. The barn is built into a hillside, which allows for efficient access to the second level hayloft. The lower level walls are unique in that they represent an early use of poured concrete.

The Cottonwood Canyon Barn was built by Harlie Ayers in 1915. Mr. Ayers was originally from Bakersfield, Vermont, and may have seen some polygon barns before moving out West. He purchased land and water rights in 1912, built his house in 1914, and put up the barn the following year (Figure II.14.1). Mr. Ayers proudly displayed a sign on the south side that stated, "Minnehaha Ranch, H.H. Ayers." Unfortunately, over the ensuing 100 years, the sign has faded away. Originally, the barn was painted bright red with white corner boards. All window and door trim were painted white, while the crowning cupola was painted the reverse: white with red corner boards. The colors, although faded, are still apparent today. A small milk house or separator room/shed was added onto the south side of the lower level (Figures II.14.1 and II.14.2)

The barn geometry is unique to the state of Washington as it is the only decagon barn with a segmented clear span hayloft without any central support. The structural roof framing pattern and space in the hayloft are quite stunning and it is hard to imagine how Mr. Ayers was able to construct such a vertical structure (Figure II.14.3). It must have been quite a delightful moment when the central scaffolding was removed to expose the clear span and space of the loft. Since the loft level had ground access, the hay was able to be easily brought in through two large doors on the uphill side of the barn. The walls of the loft are 24 feet high and provide for an abundance of hay storage for the cold winters. Mr. Ayers installed a large hay fork on a cable system to efficiently move the hay to three openings (trap doors) in the floor to feed the cows and cattle below (Figures II.14.4 and II.14.5). The roof beams are 35 feet from the walls to the center and the pattern integrates with the compression ring and cupola in the center (Figure II.14.6).

Along with the Steinke and Hall brothers' barns, the ground level surrounding walls are poured concrete. They have a stone character revealing that Mr. Ayers used a lot of fairly large round stones in the mix (probably to save the amount and cost of cement).[32] (See Figures II.14.4 and II.14.5)

In addition to this barn, Yakima—the name derived from the original Yakama Nation today living south of the city—has been known as a progressive community. While many other cities built shopping malls on the edges of their population centers, encouraging costly, auto-driven suburban sprawl, Yakima built a shopping mall in the center of its city to retain the focus of having a distinct city center. This was actually quite successful until the establishment of the "big box" stores (Walmart, Costco, Home Depot, and others) that eroded the centrality and focus of the downtown area as has happened in many cities nationwide. Yakima was also one of the first cities to build greenways with parks, walkways, and bike trails along the Yakima River and its flood plain. The city has escaped the fate of far too many other cities that built in their flood plains, requiring expensive dikes and levee systems or experiencing huge property damage during ever-increasing flood seasons caused by the changing climate from global warming.

Yakima also had one of the earliest micro-breweries in the state, which was opened by Bert Grant in the 1980s. Bert was a brew master from Scotland; he moved to Yakima to establish his personal formulas into a successful small micro-brewery. The region is known for growing quality hops and grains, important ingredients for superior brewing. Grant's Pub, Brewery and Restaurant is located in the old, restored Yakima train station in the downtown area (Figures II.14.7 and II.14.8). The original label on Bert Grant's Celtic Ale has a profound statement. We have paraphrased it a bit to apply to this volume:

Figures II.14.1 and II.14.2: Top: The Minnehaha/Ayers Barn (now known as the McGraph Barn). Note the white corner boards. The small milk house or shed is on the lower right. Bottom: Aerial view of the Minnehaha/Ayers/McGraph barn. When the barn was built, the houses below the barn (to the south) did not exist, giving a clear view of the barn and American flag sign from Cottonwood Canyon Road. (Google Maps)

> Great times make great friends. Great friends make great neighborhoods. Great neighborhoods make great cities. Great cities make great nations. Great nations make a great world. Therefore, the greatness of the world depends on…[those who preserve our historic heritage and the natural and rural environment for future generations.]

We used this insightful saying (minus the ale, of course) as an important guide to our lives and in our teaching (Figures II.14.9 and II.14.10).

Figures II.14.3, II.14.4, and II.14.5: Top: Interior of the second floor (hayloft). Note the clear span (without any central support) and beautiful framing of the roof leading to the central cupola. The star-like light pattern in the roof indicates the need for repair to prevent water damage to the structure. (This photo is a composite of two photographs.) Bottom: The lower level for the cows and cattle.

Figure II.14.6: The view of the cupola and the beautiful 10-sided framing of the roof pattern, which integrates well with the compressing ring and cupola in the center.

Figures II.14.7 and II.14.8: The historic sign on the barn from the Washington State Heritage Barn Register, and a weathered but beautiful flag painted on a 4 by 8-foot sheet of plywood on the barn. The flag has 50 stars and therefore must have been painted and installed after 1959, when Alaska became the 50th state.

Figures II.14.9 and II.14.10: Grant's original Celtic Ale and intriguing label.

15. Crocker Ranch Polygon Barn, 1915

The Crocker Barn is the only tetradecagon (14-sided) barn in the state. It is used for horses and cattle with four central columns supporting the two-segment roof.

Location: 366 Simcoe Mountain Road, Centerville, Klickitat County, Washington

Original use: Horse and cattle barn with a central manger for hay

Current use: The first level is used for horses and the loft is open and home to a barn owl.

Characteristics: The 14-sided, tetradecagon barn is 52 feet in diameter with a conical gambrel (two-segment) roof. The polygon retains the functional advantages of a round barn while the straight linear segments of the walls and roof create a more economic and efficient construction. There are four central columns extending up to support the roof. A beautiful, custom-crafted 14-sided wood cupola creates a fitting crown to the dome and provides light and important ventilation.

The Crocker barn is the only 14-sided barn in the state. In actuality, the more segments that exist to create a round form, the closer to a true circular round shape it will be, as opposed to an eight-, ten-, or twelve-sided structure. It is highly prized by the Crocker family and with the help of the Washington Heritage Barn Program and Washington State matching grants for historic preservation, the barn has been well maintained (Figure II.15.1)

The Crocker family homesteaded in Centerville along with four other Finnish families in 1887. The Crockers' original Finnish name was Kaarakka, which has a similar sound to Crocker. The four families left Finland together in the 1870s, during a terrible famine in their homeland, and homesteaded on adjacent 160-acre plots. It is interesting to note that their homestead agreement required them to plant forty acres of trees for wood and wildlife and maintain them for ten years before they were given the deed to the land. Only five acres of trees still remain from the original forty.[33] (Figure II.15.2)

Requiring woodlands is an ideal policy in light of today's global warming crisis when trees are so critical for absorbing CO_2 due to our extensive dependency on fossil fuels. The fact that their land purchase agreement from well over 100 years ago required those 40 acres be set aside for trees, possibly orchards, for nature and wildlife demonstrates their insight into how, even at that time, we can, and must, preserve the natural world around us and move to regenerative and sustainable systems. With that mindset, we can imagine that if the Crockers were still actively farming here today, they might be taking advantage of the renewable wind power available from nearby wind farms in the Centerville area.

The barn was built by John Crocker and his wife, Sara, in 1915 with the help of Peter Ahola, a carpenter and son of one of the four Finnish families who migrated with them to Centerville. At that time, constructing the barn cost $3,200. Later, a rectangular addition was added to increase the capacity of the barn.[34] (Figures II.15.3–5)

Stanley Crocker, John and Sara's son, and his wife Noreen, lived on the farm after John and Sara retired. Stanley took great pride in the barn and his cattle and horses, winning numerous awards, competitions in rodeos, and even a few horse races (Figures II.15.6–7)

Figure II.15.1: Exterior view of the Crocker Ranch round barn today. Note the basketball backboard on the wall to the right of center.

Figure II.15.2: Aerial view of the Crocker Ranch, homestead, and round barn. (Google Maps)

We were fortunate to visit the Crocker Barn in 2017 when Stanley's son and granddaughter kindly showed us the barn (and the resident barn owl). The young granddaughter stated with great charm that she wanted to be married in the barn. After exploring and photographing it, we had a chance to meet Stanley, then 97 years young (Figure II.15.8), who enthusiastically told us several fun stories about the barn's history. He asked us why we thought his father decided to build a round barn. We, of course, thought it was because of its strength and known efficiency in caring for the animals. But

Figures II.15.3, II.15.4, and II.15.5: Top: Interior view of the upper floor (mow or hayloft) and the beautifully supported dome and central cupola for light and ventilation. The photo is an integration of three photographs; the right side of the image is mirrored from the original image on the left. Compare with Figure II.15.9 where, in 1981, there was considerable buckling in the central columns. Bottom: Interior views of the lower floor of the barn in 2017 (the right side is a mirror image of the left).

Figures II.15.6 and II.15.7: The repair of the Crocker barn, roof sheathing, new asphalt shingles, and Stanley Crocker repainting.

"no," he stated with a sparkle in his eyes: "it was because his father didn't want anyone peeing in the corners!" Unfortunately, Stanley passed away in 2020 at the age of 100. He was a delightful person, actively involved in many community and animal husbandry organizations, as well as being active in numerous sports. In his high school senior year, he was the state's basketball scoring leader.[35] While attending Washington State University, he may have played on their basketball team. It is fun to think of him swooshing a round, spherical ball through a round hoop in a round barn.

Figures II.15.8, II.15.9 and II.15.10: On the left, Stanley Crocker telling stories of his life, his cats, prized horses, and his love for his family's round barn. In the middle, a 1981 photo of the buckling vertical column (before being straightened) and a round practice basketball hoop. On the right, vertical view of the central four columns and opening, which allowed hay and oats to be dropped down to the ground floor. The steel rods were added to correct the buckling in the columns.

16. Hardin Polygon Barn, 1915

The geometry of this barn is unique in the state as all other polygon barns are regular polygons with equal sides. This is the only barn with an irregular long flat side that accommodates a pair of large sliding doors.

Location: For privacy reasons, the current owner of this barn has requested that the location not be revealed.

Original use: Apple packing and storage

Current use: Equipment and storage

Characteristics: The barn has two floors and is rather unusual in that it is an irregular oval-shaped, dodecadon with unequal sides. It appears to have a longer front with large sliding doors. It has a beautifully segmented roof that integrates the unequal sides and a crowning cupola. The owner has replaced the shingles with a good asphalt shingle roof—a most important improvement to maintain the integrity of the structure.

The barn was built by Frank Hardin in 1915. The Hardins originally came from Minnesota and established a large 60- to 70-acre apple orchard. Although it is quite unusual to build a polygon barn for an apple orchard,[36] the Hardins may have been influenced by a large number of dairy barns built during this time in Minnesota, Wisconsin, Illinois, and Indiana. The apple orchard no longer exists, and the current owner has requested that we not publish his name.

The barn's geometry is unique in the state of Washington, as all the other barns are either round or regular polygons with equal sides (Figure II.16.1). The irregular long side effectively accommodated a pair of large sliding doors for sorting and storing their apples. As shown in Figure II.16.2, the barn has a single gable roof extension to allow light to the second level.

We first became aware of the barn's existence when we viewed a watercolor painting in the Northwest Museum of Art and Culture (formerly the Cheney Cowles Museum) in Spokane some forty years ago. We wish we had either purchased the painting or taken a photograph of it at the time. Even though the painting defined the general region of the barn, we searched for it for many years without success. We even wrote to the WSU agricultural extension agent for the county without any resolution. (We actually wrote to all the county agricultural extension agents throughout the state asking for the locations of round barns while researching this book.) With determination to solve this particular mystery, we finally ended up spending many hours poring over Google Maps in search of a round form in the rural agricultural landscape and we eventually located it.

In 2016, we tried to locate a phone number for the owner without success. In light of that, we decided to visit the farm. Unfortunately, the owner was quite busy and asked us to make prearrangements and return another time. Later, when we inquired into visiting the barn, we were told the owner did not want to release any information and specifically requested we keep its location private. Honoring that request, we have not given any specific location and have edited and removed all adjacent buildings and references from the photographs. Although we cannot reveal the barn's location, we can say that the lighter walls exhibit a nicely poetic harmony with the picturesque rural landscape, similar to our memory of the watercolor painting mentioned earlier.

We would love to observe the framing underneath the roof. It is the only round barn in the state that we have not been able to carefully investigate or view the interior. We remain ever hopeful that someday we will be able to do so. It is a positive sign that the current owners have installed a new roof, indicating an interest in and willingness to preserve it. It is also the single most important strategy to prevent rain, snow, and weather from penetrating the roof sheathing and decaying the structure. That single act alone should ensure the barn's continuation for another generation to come.

Figure II.16.1: The Hardin Barn. Photo has been edited to disguise the location.

Figure II.16.2: The Hardin Barn. Note the large sliding door on this front side. Photo has been edited to disguise the location.

17. Middleburg/Burge/Deep Creek Round Barn, 1916

This unique barn is the only barn in the state designed with a cork floor for the cows to stand on. The softer surface was intended to insulate them from the cold, hard concrete slab.

Location: N 811 Deep Creek Road, Medical Lake, Spokane County, Washington

Original use: Dairy barn with a silo in the center

Current use: Burge Private Museum of Western Antiques and Saddles

Characteristics: Circular round with a central silo and original T-extension. It has a conical-shaped (hip) roof with the central silo extending above the roof. It is 60 feet in diameter. It was originally designed as a dairy barn on the lower level with hayloft around the silo on the second level.

Mr. M.F. Middleburg purchased the farm in 1911 and constructed the barn in 1916 (Figures II.17.1 and II.17.2). The reasoning for the round barn is unknown but it was carefully planned and constructed as a dairy barn following the layout discussed and illustrated in the publications of that time. There is a close similarity in size and form to the Manning round barn built in 1901 some 75 miles south between Colfax and Pullman. Any influence or family ties are not known. To celebrate his proud accomplishment, he hosted a barn dance for his family and neighbors. It surely must have been fun doing circular dance movements in the round form.

Middleburg planned the barn for 35 cows. Feeding the cows was quite efficient with the silo in the middle and milking stalls radiating from the day-lit outer circle. He also installed a cork floor where the cows would stand on softer surfaces and be insulated from the cold hard concrete slab. We wonder if his contented cows produced more milk.

The barn had the recommended sanitation system where the manure would be washed into a continuous gutter in the floor and then channeled the "tailings" through a drain line, to be stored for fertilizing the fields in the spring (Figures II.17.5 and II.17.6). The barn was also originally lit by carbide lanterns (Figures II.17.9 and II.17.10), another rather unusual innovation.[37]

Ed and Sally Burge purchased the farm in 1975 and have lovingly maintained the barn since that time. In 2005, the first floor was converted into a private museum for western antiques featuring their extensive collection of saddles. If interested in a visit, it is important to call first to make arrangements (Figures II.17.7 and II.17.8).

We have visited the Deep Creek Farm and barn three times. The first time, Tom and his sister Joan, who was visiting from Illinois, found it located relatively close to the Spokane International Airport. The second visit was with architecture students interested in historic preservation, and the third visit occurred in 2015.

Being able to see the progressive changes in the barn was inspiring. In the 1980s, the barn was used for storage, some hay in the loft, while the lower floor was waiting for a special use (Figures II.17.3 and II.17.4). Fortunately, in 2005, Ed and Sally Burge converted the barn into the museum for their extensive collection. Although the original use was for cows, this is a perfectly fitting reuse for such a special building. Sally states the barn is in excellent shape; all they have done through the years is to re-roof and paint this noble structure. We dearly appreciate Ed and Sally's kindness in allowing us to visit and see their special farm, barn, and museum.

In 2015, over Memorial Day weekend, the Burges permitted the Washington Civil War Society to set up an encampment and stage four battles, allowing some 5,000 visitors to experience the camp as well as their museum. We sincerely regret we could not be one of those visitors; hopefully we can attend another year (Figures II.17.9–11).

Figure II.17.1: The Deep Creek round barn in 2015.

Figure II.17.2: Aerial view of the Deep Creek farm and round barn. (Google Maps)

Figures II.17.3 and II.17.4: The Deep Creek Barn second-level loft, with a silo in the center (left, 1980, and right, 2015).

Figures II.17.5 and II.17.6: The Deep Creek Barn ground floor in 1980 (right) as a working barn and in 2015 (left) as a private Museum of Western Antiques and Saddles. The gutter in the floor was the sanitation system: the manure was washed out through drains (shown in lower part of Figure II.17.6) and was used to fertilize the fields. The area with the saddles and new wall on the right was where the cows would stand for milking and feeding around the inner ring, with the silo in the center.

Figures II.17.7 and II.17.8: Left: The inner second ring is where the cows would be fed around the silo (wall on the right). Right: A view into the silo—now used in the museum to feature a beautiful wood horse and the family's extensive trophy collection.

Figures II.17.9, II.17.10 and II.17.11: Above: The original carbide lanterns, another rather unique innovation. Below: The Farm's welcoming sign.

18. Gallaher Round Barn, circa 1916–1920s
(and octagon house, 1914)

These two structures (the circular round barn and the 8-sided octagonal house) are the only combination of a round barn and house in the state. Both structures were built by the Gallaher brothers.

Location: 12 miles northwest of Mansfield, Douglas County, Washington

Original use: Horse and cattle barn

Current use: Barn burned down in the 1920s; house still stands.

Characteristics: The barn was originally designed for the farm's working horses and some cattle on the lower level with a hayloft on the second level. It was a true, circular round barn approximately 80 feet in diameter with a curved dome roof. It had distinctive circular patterns painted around the windows and doors.

♦

In 1920, brothers Doss and Clyde Gallaher moved from Tennessee to a homestead near Mansfield, Washington (similar to the Hall brothers, pp. 45–49). When the Gallaher brothers married and started their families, they established their homes just a few miles apart. Around 1916, Doss, with Clyde's help, built this distinctive, large round barn (Figure II.18.1). Like the early round barns of the Palouse region, the barn was used for horses to supply the literal "horsepower" for farming and transportation. The homestead and barn also had some cattle. Doss was quite proud of the fact that the horses with carriages and other farm equipment could go into the barn, circle around and come out the same door without backing up or having to turn around.[38] The Gallahers' pride in the barn was also expressed in the circles painted to accent the windows and doors (See Figure II.18.1).

It is truly unfortunate that the barn burned down shortly after it was built. It was almost lost to the historical record, but thanks to the Mansfield Historic Museum, we have been allowed to include herein the only photograph of the barn known to exist.

This structure was the last round barn we discovered in the state. In late July 2020, we were watching the local news and saw an extensive field fire just west of Mansfield. In the photograph shown on the news, we thought we saw a round barn in the distant background. To satisfy our curiosity, we called numerous people in Mansfield to inquire about the possible barn. The fire department, the Grange, and even the school superintendent all stated there was no round barn in the fire zone. The school superintendent suggested we call the mayor of Mansfield, Tom Snell. Mayor Snell

confirmed everyone's statements and mentioned there are numerous large rocks that form circular patterns in the landscape and thought that might have been what we observed (Figure II.18.2).

Satisfied with the inquiry, we almost ended our discussion when the mayor asked why we were so interested in round barns. We briefly explained our research and he then told us there had been a round barn northwest of Mansfield that burned down in the 1920s. Surprised, we asked if there was any information on the barn or the family. He said that the family moved soon after their barn and home burned down but a photograph of the barn was kept in their town museum. He kindly offered to meet us at the museum and said he would gladly open it for us to see the photograph. As we were too far away for a quick visit, he arranged to

Figure II.18.1: A historic photo of the exterior of the Gallaher Barn, with Doss Gallaher painting the unique circle on the doorway and three of their eight children on the horse. Photo courtesy of the Mansfield Museum.

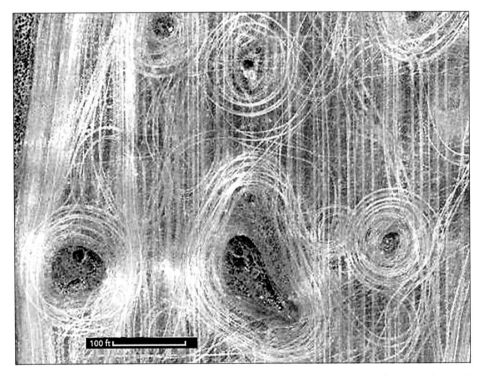

Figure II.18.2: Aerial image of the fields around Mansfield showing the extent of the "circular" rock formations in the fields created by the tracks of farm equipment. (Google Maps).

have a copy of the photo sent to us. Thank you, Mayor Snell, and Diane Michelson, for sending the delightful photograph of this unique, true-round barn. Unfortunately, our search and discussions with the Gallaher family also concludes that this is the only known photograph of the barn. It is ironic that an extensive grassland fire brought forth our knowledge of the barn that, sadly, was also destroyed by a fire.

Doss's brother, Clyde, helped construct and eventually lived in a fascinating octagonal house built in 1913–1914 just a mile or so away (Figure II.18.3). James Kinney, a carpenter, designed and built this truly unique house and gave it to his daughter, Ruth, when she and Clyde Gallaher married.[39] James Kinney and family were pioneering homesteaders who moved to this area in 1889, the year Washington became the forty-second state.[40] Kinney had a sawmill and cut the lumber from trees on his land to construct the home. The house was an amazing design for the time; it was innovative, and all of its crafted details were cut by hand.[41]

The house has been referred to as "the house of many gables" (16 in total). There are eight main gables, one for each bedroom on the second floor, while the other eight, smaller gables above provided panoramic views and light for the unfinished, unused third floor. Alternate bedroom doors had glass panels to provide light into the central spiral staircase.[42] The unused third floor could have made a delightful office or studio and would function like a sundial, with light moving throughout the day from the eastern sunrise to the western sunset.

In 1936, all the Gallaher children had moved except for the eldest son, Huston, who inherited the house. He and his family lived in it for a short time while building a more "modern" home. In 1940, R.B. "Bunny" Allen visited the abandoned house and attempted to buy it, but Huston wasn't ready to sell at that time. The house remained empty and continued to weather unoccupied, but Allen persisted, eventually being allowed to purchase and save the unusual home. Allen contracted to move the house some twenty-three highway miles to Bridgeport, WA, in 1993 (Figure II.18.4). As the crow flies, it ended up only five miles from its original homestead location. Thousands of people watched it cross the Columbia River Bridge into Bridgeport. Nine feet of the roof had to be temporarily removed just to get it across the bridge.

The Allens restored it to the original character, updating electrical and

Figure II.18.3: The just-completed Gallaher house in its original location northwest of Mansfield, Washington. Photo courtesy of the Mansfield Museum.

water systems, and getting it listed on the National Register of Historic Places.[43] More recently, the house was purchased by Barbara Magers. She completed a lot of restorative interior design work, furnishing it with appropriate antiques of the period. Mary Ellen (Gallaher) Wax states that Ms.

Magers gave her a tour of the house: they shared tea as she reminisced of visiting her grandmother there and playing on the circular stairs and exploring the attic.[44] Thank you to both Mr. and Mrs. Allen, as well as Ms. Magers, for preserving such a fascinating part of our historical heritage.

Figure II.18.4: The Gallaher octagonal house moved to the current Bridgeport location in 1993.

19. Yochum Ranch Round Barn, 1954

Due to its unique location on an upper plateau, this barn was deliberately designed as a low-profile round to withstand the 100-mph winds that frequent this area.

Location: 26126 Peola Road, 15 miles west of Clarkston Heights on Highway 128, Asotin County, Washington

Original use: The barn was built for dairy cows

Current use: Storage

Characteristics: The barn is a true round, 57 feet in diameter with a 22-foot-diameter feeding area in the center. It has an upper story hayloft, which effectively supplies the central manger below and a round, domed roof and crowning wooden cupola that provides critically important ventilation. The clear span roof framing creates a beautiful, uninterrupted dome ceiling and roof. The barn was designed to have an intentional low profile to resist the strong winds that crossed the upper plateau in the winter.

Ed Yochum and his family homesteaded the "Pleasant Ridge" area and established the Yochum Ranch. Ed and his son, Roger, built this 57-foot diameter round barn in 1954 (Figure II.19.1).[45] Both Ed and Roger were fascinated by unique construction projects. One of their first was a large log community gathering and dance hall, which stood along Peola Road for years (Figures II.19.11 and II.19.12). They also constructed two 40-foot-diameter water cisterns and a round chicken coop on their ranch before building the barn (Figure II.19.2).

Figure II.19.1: The Yochum round barn in 2015.

Figure II.19.2: Aerial view of the Yochum ranch in 2016. The 57-foot-diameter round barn is located in the bottom center, the two 40-foot-diameter water cisterns are seen on the upper and lower left and a small round chicken coop is on the upper right. (Google Maps)

Figure II.19.3: This photo shows the beautiful radial frame and central light coming from the cupola.

The Yochum barn is a true round barn and not a polygon form, which had become more popular earlier in the century. The barn was intentionally designed to be round as well as having a low profile in order to withstand the strong winds (sometimes reaching as high as 100 mph) that occur on this upper plateau. The Yochums cut their own timber from a nearby forest; 90 poles were used as beams in the upper floor alone. They also prefabricated the upper curved and laminated roof beams from milled 1-inch boards on the ground prior to lifting them into place (Figures II.19.3–6).

We discovered and photographed the Yochum barn and the dance hall in 1974. We returned again in 2015 with our son, Jon. At that time, we arranged to meet with Roger Yochum who was quite gracious at the young age of 79, to take the time to talk with us about his beloved family ranch and barn.[46] He discussed his family's history and the challenges of homesteading on the high plateau and emphasized their love for the construction of unique buildings. They began their collection of unusual structures by moving, and adaptively reusing, a rural church that became their original home. They enjoyed the creative challenges of designing and constructing the polygon community dance hall out of logs (Figures II.19.11 and II.19.12), then moved on to the building of the two round water cisterns, and finally, concluded with their round barn—the challenging geometry and low profile selected to resist the strong winds of the plateau.

Mr. Yochum emphasized that everything was hand done, including harvesting the logs for the second story of the barn from a forest located just west of the ranch. In just two days, they hand cut the 90 logs for the beams needed to construct the second floor, strong enough to hold the 40 tons of hay required to feed the animals through the harsh winter months (Figure II.19.7). We asked what the trailer was used for, and he proudly explained that they designed it to plant seedlings for the U.S. Forest Service to gain additional income for the ranch. They could plant 1,000 trees per hour with that machine (Figures II.19.8–10). We owe a thank you to Ed and Roger Yochum for replanting our forests and helping to reduce global warming.

Figures II.19.4, II.19.5, and II.19.6: Upper photo shows the upper hayloft and domed roof with feed manger below. The lower photos show the lower level (the image on the right is a mirrored image of the original photo on the left).

Figure II.19.7: Roger Yochum leading the way to the barn on his 4-wheeler.

Figures II.19.8, II.19.9, and II.19.10: Left image, the tree planting trailer; middle image, discarded nursery containers in which the trees were delivered; right image, discussing the barn construction in the barn's doorway.

Figures II.19.11 and II.19.12: On the left, the painting of the community dance hall is proudly displayed in Mr. Yochum's home, and right, a photograph of the structure in 1974.

20. Wagner Polygon Barn, 1971

The octagonal Wagner Barn is the only round barn in the state to be protected by a land conservancy. It is owned by The Western River Conservancy of Portland, Oregon, and is an important part of the Yakama Nation Upper Columbia Habitat Project.

Location: Five miles north of Winthrop on Eastside Chewuch Road, Winthrop, Okanagan County, Washington

Original use: The barn was built for mules and horses used as pack animals for groups who wanted to adventure deep into the beautiful Methow Valley and the eastern side of the Cascade Mountains.

Current use: The barn is used for a few horses and periodically for community events.

Characteristics: The barn is an eight-sided octagon, 61 feet in diameter with a mezzanine/hayloft circulating around the upper story and an open atrium in the center. The barn has a conical single segmented hip roof with gables at the front and back entries. The gables provide access to the mezzanine for loading hay for the animals. The barn is crowned with a metal roof with four skylights and a small octagon cupola (providing critically important ventilation) with a beautiful weathervane.

T he design of the Wagner Barn is said to have been patterned after the Stewart Barn in Mazama, Washington, some eight miles to the north of the Wagner Ranch. (Discussed further in the following section, the Stewart Half-Polygon Barn was only a half of an octagon and sadly burned down, along with the homestead, in 1963.) The Wagners built their barn in 1971 for housing mules and horses for visitors who wanted to backpack and explore this remote and scenic part of Washington (Figure II.20.1). This chapter considers not only a unique barn but also the restoration of a historic town and the saving of a river (Figure II.20.2).

The Wagners owned and managed a large sawmill near Twisp, some ten miles north. They were very active members of the Winthrop community and donated resources to the town to build a community swimming pool and a ski lodge as well as fostering an interest in recreating the town into a realistic historic "western" downtown—all important aspects in preserving our natural, rural, and cultural heritage. Because the surrounding North Cascade Mountains are so rugged and scenic, the state petitioned Congress to declare it a National Park. It has some 342 glaciers (due to climate change, however, most are receding) and is commonly known as the United States' Switzerland. The first request to declare it a National Park came in 1892 and numerous other subsequent attempts failed until finally, in 1968, the North Cascades National Park was created.

It is Washington state's third National Park.[47] Highway 20 was constructed through the park, connecting to the Methow Valley and Winthrop. Due to heavy snowfall, the scenic highway through the park is closed during winter months.

When Highway 20 is open, the eastern access or egress from the Park goes through the Methow Valley and Winthrop. The Wagners, along with the community, planned to make Winthrop a destination town. To that end, they created the Shafer Historical Museum and restored the "western" town characteristics to preserve the historic and cultural "spirit of the valley."[48]

Fortunately, in 2018, the 328-acre Wagner Ranch with its barn (Figures

II.20.3 and II.20.4) was bought by The Western River Conservancy of Portland, Oregon, for $3.3 million. The conservancy's goal is to preserve and restore the rivers in the Pacific Northwest for fish spawning and their habitat (primarily salmon, steelhead, and trout). Their website states, "sometimes to save a river, you have to buy it." The property, along with others, is to be an important part of the Yakama Nation Upper Columbia Habitat Restoration Project.[49] The barn will be maintained, along with the property and, the protected Chewuch River (Figure II.20.5)

Figure II.20.1: Exterior of the Wagner barn in 2019 during a celebration of the conservancy. Photo courtesy of Don Nelson, editor of the *Methow Valley Newspaper*.

Figure II.20.2: Aerial view of the Wagner ranch and farm with the octagonal barn in lower center, a four-sided home above it, and a six-sided (hexagonal) home in the upper left. (Google Maps)

Figure II.20.3: Beautiful roof framing, central cupola and four skylights. Photo courtesy of Stephen Mitchell, Cascade Outdoor Group, LLC.

Figure II.20.4: Interior of the barn showing the surrounding mezzanine. Photo courtesy of Stephen Mitchell, Cascade Outdoor Group, LLC.

Figure II.20.5: The Wagner barn before the metal roof was installed. Photograph by Bob and Dorothy Dunham.

21. Stewart Half-Polygon Barn, 1914–1963

The Stewart Barn is a one-of-a-kind "half of a polygon" (octagon) barn that was built as an addition onto a rectangular barn.

Location: Mazama, Okanogan County, Washington

Original use: The barn was built for dairy cows and some horses. Most of the horses were used to plow, plant and harvest the farmland.

Current use: The barn burned down in 1963.

Characteristics: The barn was half of an eight-sided octagon attached to the long side of a rectangular barn. It combined the efficiency of a polygon barn with the ease of construction and utility of a rectangular barn. Stewart's design of the polygon segment also had unique ventilation louvers for the second story hayloft. The louvers accented the wall-to-roof connection, making the roof look like it was floating above the walls. It was a prized feature in the Methow Valley and it is thought to be the prototype for the Wagner barn, eight miles southeast of Mazama (five miles northwest of Winthrop), built in 1970–71.[50]

The Stewart Barn was a one-of-a-kind structure that combined an octagonal half-polygon portion with a more traditional prow-front rectangular barn located in the picturesque Methow Valley. The Stewart family homesteaded on 160 acres near Mazama in the 1890s. They lived in a log cabin and later built a comfortable two-story farmhouse.

They constructed the barn in 1914 (Figure II.21.1) with the help of a carpenter, Henry Biart. John A. (Jack) Stewart was a mining engineer who loved prospecting in many areas in the Methow Valley and surrounding mountain ranges. He was a rather proactive engineer, having developed a lumber mill that served the early settlement in the area, and he was a proud user of a camera. The historic photographs shown here were taken and developed by him.

After the barn was completed, Jack and his wife, Minnie, started an active dairy farm. The polygon portion of the barn housed some 30 dairy cows with a hayloft above (Figures II.21.2 and II.21.3) The Stewarts retired in 1944 and, unfortunately, the barn, home, and other structures burned down in 1963.[51]

II.21.1: The Stewart half-octagon barn connected to the rectangular barn. In the middle of the photo an "elephant" shaped bale of hay is being lifted into the second-story loft. Photograph courtesy of the Shafer Historical Museum photograph archive, Winthrop, Washington.

Figures II.21.2: Note the ventilation louvers under the roof—accenting the wall-to-roof connection. Photograph courtesy of the Shafer Historical Museum photograph archive, Winthrop, Washington.

Figure II.21.3: The Stewart homestead: a two-story home and half-octagon barn connected to a rectangular barn under construction in 1914. Photograph courtesy of the Shafer Historical Museum photograph archive, Winthrop, Washington.

NOTES

1. https://dahp.wa.gov/historic-registers/heritage-barn-register

2. Nutter Barn. Historic Property Inventory Report, 12 May 2015. Heritage Barn Register, Department of Archaeology and Historic Preservation, State of Washington (Olympia, Washington, 12 May 2015)

3. Cowlitz Round Barn Preservation Association. "A Treasure from the Past, A Future Legacy." Cowlitz Round Barn Preservation Association (Bend, Oregon).

4. Wilkins, P. "For Love of a Barn," in *Somewhere in the Northwest: On the Road in Oregon and Washington.* Bear Creek Press (Wallowa, Oregon: 2004).

5. Toor, Karen and Ron Towner. "The Hall Round Barn: Ethnoarchaeology in Whitman Co., WA." Report for Dr. Ackerman, Anthropology 536, Washington State University (Pullman, Washington: 1983).

6. Holstine, C. "Max Steinke's Round Barn." *Bunchgrass Historian,* Whitman County Historical Society (Colfax, Washington: 17 (3), Fall 1989) p. 13.

7. Chandler, H. "Historic Round Barn Razed: The Novel Structure was the Last Word in Design Half a Century Ago." *Bunchgrass Historian*, Whitman County Historical Society (Colfax, Washington: 30 (2), 2004).

8. Holstine, C. "Max Steinke's Round Barn." *Bunchgrass Historian,* Whitman County Historical Society (Colfax, Washington, V17(3), Fall 1989) p. 13.

9. Holstine, C. "Max Steinke's Round Barn."

10. Phone interview with Mark Hall on 26 April 2019.

11. Toor, Karen and Ron Towner. "The Hall Round Barn: Ethnoarchaeology in Whitman Co., WA." Report for Dr. Ackerman, Anthropology 536, Washington State University (Pullman, Washington, 1983).

12. Weddell, Jim. "Round Barns of the Palouse." MS Report, Department of Architecture, Washington State University (Pullman, Washington, ca. 1977).

13. Comments from Renee Simmerman, personal visit in 2014.

14. Leonard, George. "The Leonard Barn." Personal notes prepared by George M. Leonard (Pullman, Washington, 5 February 1975).

15. Burger, David Mark and Nys, Eric Steven. "T.A. Leonard Barn," Pullman, Whitman County, Washington. Historic American Buildings Survey (HABS) No. WA168, 1985. Prints and Photographs Division (Library of Congress, Washington D.C., 1985).

16. https://sah-archipedia.org/buildings/WA-01-075-0015.

17. McDonald, L. "*Where Washingtonians Lived.*" Superior Publishing Co. (Seattle, WA, 1969).

18. "The Coffman Carriage House and Barn." *The Chehalis Bee Nugget* (Chehalis, Washington, 25 December 1908)

19. Frazier, Wm. Heritage Barn Register, Department of Archaeology and Historic Preservation, State of Washington (Olympia, Washington)

20. Frazier, Wm. Heritage Barn Register

21. Personal discussion with William Frazier, 2018

22. https://en.wikipedia.org/wiki/Drew_Bledsoe

23. Personal phone interview with Dale Duskin on 11 April 2019.

24. Personal phone interview with Dale Duskin on 11 April 2019.

25. Martin, Irene, *Skamokawa: Sad Years, Glad Years* (self-published, 1985).

26. Martin, Irene, *Skamokawa: Sad Years, Glad Years*

27. Majors, Harry M., *Exploring Washington*, Van Winkle Publishing (Holland, MI: 1975).

28. Majors, Harry M., *Exploring Washington*

29. Martin, Irene, *Skamokawa: Sad Years, Glad Years*

30. Martin, Irene, *Skamokawa: Sad Years, Glad Years*

31. Martin, Irene, *Skamokawa: Sad Years, Glad Years*

32. Personal notes sent to us from the McGraph family.

33. https://dahp.wa.gov/sites/default/files/Barnbook%20ID3.pdf

34. Ibid

35. https://www.goldendalesentinel.com/story/2020/04/08/obituaries/stanley-wilbert-crocker/12996.html

36. Massengale, D. "Community Cultural Resource Survey," 1980.

37. Personal handout from Ed and Sally Burge.

38. Interview and correspondence from Mary Ellen (Gallaher) Wax, July 2020.

39. The Gallaher House, National Register of Historic Places, Mansfield, Douglas County, Washington (U.S. Department of the Interior, National Park Service, Washington D.C.)

40. Interview and correspondence with Adele Gallaher Drummond.

41. Nicholson, J. "Eight-Sided House on the Move" and "The House of Eight Gables." *The Star* (Grand Coulee, Washington). Date unknown; articles provided by Adele Gallaher Drummond.

42. The Gallaher House, National Register of Historic Places, Mansfield, Douglas County, Washington (U.S. Department of the Interior, National Park Service, Washington D.C.)

43. Simmuns, M. "After Decades, This Dreamer Restores His House of Many Corners." *Grit: Rural American Know How* (Topeka: Kansas, 28 August, 1914).

44. Interview and correspondence from Mary Ellen (Gallaher) Wax, July 2020.

45. Weatherly, B. "Asotin County's Round Barn." *Jawbone Flat Gazette*, Twin City Printing (Clarkston, WA, 21 May 1986).

46. Yochum, R. Personal note of our discussion in 2015

47. https://en.wikipedia.org/wiki/North_Cascades_National_Park

48. https://winthropwashington.com/history/

49. https://methowvalleynews.com/2019/07/03/wagner-stafford-ranches-preserved-for-river-habitat-restoration/

50. Notes attached to the photographs in the Shafer Historical Museum collection.

51. Personal interview with Claude Miller, 11 May 2020.

CHAPTER III

Round Barn Preservation:
Reanimated, Relocated, and Recycled

Robert F. Kennedy once said,

"Small actions can be like pebbles thrown into a still lake. Ripples of hope cascade [radiating in circles] outwards and change the world."

As discussed in the introduction and throughout this work, unique barns and farms are an important part of the cultural heritage, agricultural history, and beauty inherent in the rural landscape. It is indeed understandable, yet sad, when these historic barns collapse, due to time, wear and weather, and changes in technology and farming practices, ultimately dissolving into rural ruins. It is encouraging to see some barns being well-maintained or restored and still standing or even moved and reanimated into new uses. Fortunately, there are support options available from various local and state organizations to help with their maintenance and preservation.

Through the years, as we have visited, studied, and loved these barns—and have watched the demise of too many—we have realized that the barns have taught us many lessons. We have been impressed with not only their extraordinary beauty and structural integrity, but also the ways in which they have contributed to their communities and are integral to our country's development and rural heritage. As we observed some disappearing, it struck us just how vital it is that we not only use these vanishing resources, but care for them in a way that prevents their loss to future generations.

These barns expanded our awareness to the importance of preservation in some very profound ways. The next two chapters feature examples of barns—some round and some rectangular—that have been adaptively reused and, in several cases, even moved to other locations and reconstructed for new venues. We observed and visited many examples of unique barns that stand as living laboratories—dramatically conveying the various roles they can fill rather than being torn down. By their very nature, these examples exhibit sustainability in its highest form, saving the invested resources embodied within them—the monetary, the natural materials and labor to construct them, and the years of use that contributed to the success of the people, animals, farms, and communities they served. Those embodied resources must be saved and redirected into new and creative contemporary ways that will contribute to our communities in the future as they have in the past. They enrich our collective culture and continue to help communities find their way into a more sustainable future.

While Chapter II inventories and brings awareness to the round barns of Washington and the Pacific Northwest, there are other barns located throughout the United States that

are unique. We chose to include several of them specifically as they offer important lessons of what could be done to save these barns; they are living, functioning examples that enrich our story.

It is our hope that many of these striking barns—some would say "cathedrals" to agriculture—can and will be saved in Washington like many from other states. Prime locations for abandoned round barns could be county fairgrounds, or they could be used as the central feature of historic outdoor museums where they could move, reassemble, and restore historic buildings, equipment, and artifacts like the two discussed in South Dakota and Vermont. These could be significant learning centers for Washington's historic heritage.

Besides county fairgrounds, another appropriate location would be our prominent agricultural land-grant university, Washington State University in Pullman. In fact, WSU would be quite appropriate, considering that Whitman County has more round barns than any other county in Washington state and a beautiful, well-preserved example, the Leonard Barn, still exists today just three miles east of campus. This rural center could be tied into Idaho's land-grant university, the University of Idaho, eight miles to the east of Pullman and five miles from the Leonard barn. The University of Idaho also has some significant agricultural buildings still in use today.

In addition, Chapter IV explores a few significant rectangular barns and buildings that have been reanimated into new uses and community "green" activities that can help save a bit of our history and the planet. These structures are important examples of preservation, adaptive reuse, and sustainability. We identify some of the people who have had the will and wisdom to save these unique and irreplaceable aspects of our culture and world. As this is just a brief summary, there are many others yet to be discovered. We invite you to come explore with us as we contemplate our future.

French Round Barn, 1882
Frenchglen, Oregon

One of the first round barns in the Northwest was built on the Pete French Ranch in Frenchglen, Oregon (Figure III.1.1). The French Round Barn is not an actual barn, but rather a one-story structure for the care and training of wild horses (Figure III.1.2). It is a dramatic, 100-foot-diameter circular building with a central 60-foot-diameter corral enclosed by a full height stone wall. A 20-foot-wide circular track exists on the outer side of the stone wall (Figure III.1.3), used for breaking, training, and exercising French's extensive herd of horses,

Figure III.1.1: The French Round Barn sitting elegantly in the vast French Ranch, 1980.

Figure III.1.2: The French Round Barn, 1980.

which at times approximated upwards of 1000 head. It is thought that Pete French may have built three of these barns, but only one remains today. This barn (and possibly any others built by French) protected the horses from the harsh winter winds while training during cold weather, which is common in the high country of eastern central Oregon.[1] The barn is a unique structure and predates all but one of the barns in Washington state (the earliest being the Nutter Barn built in 1872; see pp. 21–25).

The structure is one of a kind. It is beautifully supported by a central juniper post with an umbrella-like framing connecting the roof beams (Figure III.1.4). The diagonal framing, besides creating a fan-like accent, also effectively reduces the length of span and, therefore, the size of the roof beams (Figure III.1.5). The same diagonal bracing is used in the outer ring.

In 1949, the owners at the time, Thomas and Richard Jenkins, deeded this historic barn to the Oregon Historical Society (OHS), along with two acres of land and a public access easement to this one-of-a-kind barn. In 1995, the OHS gave the barn to Oregon Parks and Recreation Department, and it now has an Information Center and is the focal point of the Pete French Round Barn State Park. The site and barn were listed on the National Register of Historic Places in 1971.[2] Thank you, Thomas and Richard Jenkins.

There exists another round horse stable/arena in Washington state that is similar to the Frenchglen structure. It was built in the 1980s and is located in the Meadow Ridge Equestrian Community in Arlington (Figure III.1.6). It, too, is 100 feet in diameter. This arena is not listed in the twenty-one historic Washington barns discussed in the previous section because it is primarily one story (with a minor mezzanine around the perimeter) and is not yet 50 years old. Although its purpose is similar to the historic Frenchglen structure, its layout is the reverse. The Frenchglen plan has a corral for the horses in the center and the training/riding track in the outer ring. The Meadow Ridge layout has its training/riding arena in the

Figure III.1.3: This image shows the inner corral within the stone wall on the left and the outer 20-foot perimeter circular track on the right. This photo was sent to us many years ago, and unfortunately, the date and photographer's name have been lost to time.

Figures III.1.4 and III.1.5: The interior central juniper column and umbrella-like framing.

center and individual private horse stalls around the perimeter (Figure III.1.7). In both barns, the horses in the corral or stalls can observe other horses being trained. The main structure and geometry of the interior 60-foot-diameter arena is a 12-sided dodecagon, but the 20-foot outer perimeter (the outermost concentric ring) for the horse stalls is subdivided, giving the exterior 24 sides, or an icositetragon. The barn's main structure is said to use timbers recycled from a commercial dock.[3] Note the addition of the skylights in the roof that adds natural daylighting in the interior arena, thereby reducing the need for supplemental energy use from electric lighting (Figure III.1.8).

Figure III.1.6: The Meadow Ridge horse stables and arena, 1989.

Figure III.1.7: Aerial view of the Meadow Ridge Equestrian Community and round barn. Note the central star-like skylights and individual perimeter skylights, one for each of the eighteen horse stalls, with individual exterior paddocks/yards. (Google Maps)

Figure III.1.8: Interior composite photograph of the central arena of the Meadow Ridge Equestrian Community barn, 1985. The image shows four of the eighteen individual horse stalls. Photo enhanced by Rob Wagoner.

Armstrong/Doncaster Round Barn, 1882

Twin Bridges, Montana

The Armstrong/Doncaster Round Barn is also commonly called the Bayer Barn (the name of the second owner) or the Round Barn at Twin Bridges. Twin Bridges is a rural farming and ranching community in southwest-ern Montana near the Yellowstone and Grand Teton National Parks. It has a population of 450 and sits in pictur-esque high mountain country at 4,626 feet above sea level (Figure III.2.1). The barn was built in 1882, the same year as the barn in Frenchglen, and had the same size and purpose: to train and protect horses from severe cold weather. Noah Armstrong, a wealthy mining entrepreneur, built the barn for his love of racehorses and named the ranch

Figure III.2.1: Distant view of the Doncaster Barn and setting in the beautiful high altitude of Jefferson Valley. Photo courtesy of Ted Catton.

after a famous English thoroughbred racehorse, Doncaster (1870–1892).[4]

Like a tiered wedding cake, the barn has three functional cascading stories (Figures III.2.2 and III.2.3). The lowest level is 100 feet in diameter with a 20-foot-wide circulator track for exercising and training the horses, especially during the cold weather. It also has 26 horse stalls around the perimeter, two hospital stalls, office space, and sleeping quarters for staff. Mr. Armstrong had designed four-foot-high fences between the stalls to encourage what he believed would be "neighborly companionship" and to relieve the monotony of indoor horse life. The center of the barn has a spiral staircase as well as an elevator to carry the grain to the second level.

The second level is 75 feet in diameter and was used to store feed for the horses during the long winters. There were individual chutes to feed each of the horse stalls. The uppermost third level is 30 feet in diameter and contained an 11,000-gallon water tank to supply gravity-fed water to the horses.

On the peak of the roof, there was a 12-foot tower and a windmill to pump the water into the tank. Unfortunately, we could not find a photograph of the windmill, which is now long gone. In Figure III.2.2, the statue of a famous horse named Spokane now sits on top of the tower.[5]

Noah Armstrong raised some famous racehorses. One, named Spokane, won many prestigious races and is the only Montana horse ever to win the Kentucky Derby and the Triple Crown, in 1889. The name Spokane is derived from the Native American tribe who lived in the Spokane region of northeastern Washington state. Spokane means "children of the sun." The city of Spokane (first called Spokane Falls, describing the Spokane River's dramatic water falls that cascade through the center of the city) was a boom town during the late nineteenth century and now is the second largest city in the state.[6] Armstrong had numerous business dealings in Spokane Falls. According to one story, he was in Spokane Falls when the horse was born; hence the name, which gave northeastern Washington considerable acclaim when the chestnut colt became world famous.[7]

Winning the Kentucky Derby is an amazing accomplishment for a horse raised and trained in the high altitude and harsh winters of Montana. Here's the story of Spokane's achievements:

> This little chestnut horse named Spokane really did accomplish something…at Churchill [Downs] in 1889. There were powerful entries that year, which included Once

Figure III.2.2: The Doncaster Barn today, restored and used as an event center. A weathervane, presumed to be the famous horse Spokane, has replaced the original windmill. Image courtesy of the Round Barn at Twin Bridges.

Figure III.2.3: The Bayer Barn and ranch used for cattle in an undated photo. The original windmill on the tower was removed. Image courtesy of the Round Barn at Twin Bridges.

Again, Bootmaker, Sportsman, Cassius, Hindoocraft, Outbound, and Proctor Knott. The odds on Spokane were 10 to 1; the odds on Proctor Knott, the favorite, were 2 to 1...

The physical contrast between Spokane and Proctor Knott was startling...Proctor Knott [was] an equine giant...Even the crowd of 20,000 people that day could easily see the contrast as they cheered Proctor Knott and laughed at Spokane as he entered the track.

As the field of horses bolted from the gate, Proctor Knott took...the lead. But Spokane, in his usual style, hung back in seventh place. Then after the turn, he began to stretch himself, moving up to fifth, and then, seemingly with ease, to third place....As the field neared the head of the stretch, Proctor Knott was still leading, but then the unbelievable happened: Spokane passed Once Again and moved up to Proctor Knott.

Stride for stride the two horses came down the stretch. Spokane's jockey had not touched the whip to his mount, but Proctor Knott's rider began using his vigorously. Not until they neared the finish line did Spokane's jockey use his stick. But one good lick did it—and with a gallant lunge, Spokane forged ahead by a nose...the little horse set a new record....

Those backing Proctor Knott clamored for another chance, and about a week later, the two horses met again in the Clark Stakes at the Downs. Again, Proctor Knott was made favorite and again, Spokane was victorious.

On June 22 at Washington Park, the horses met again. And again, Spokane beat Proctor Knott, this time winning the American Derby In July, Proctor Knott earned somewhat of a revenge over Spokane by beating him in the Sheridan Stakes at Washington Park by three lengths. But this was to be Spokane's

Figure III.2.4: The reanimated Round Barn at Twin Bridges is an event and community center. Image courtesy of the Round Barn at Twin Bridges.

Figure III.2.5: The "wedding cake" barn and venue center at Headwaters Ranch. Image courtesy of Headwaters Ranch.

last race, for he was later hurt and was unable to race again.[8]

In 1900, Armstrong sold the ranch and barn to Max Lauterbach and later it was sold to Arthur and Elizabeth Bayer, who used the barn and ranch for cattle. Unfortunately, the barn was not well maintained over the years and slowly fell into disrepair.

In 1997, the barn was sold to Allan Hamilton, who began restoration work. In 2008, the barn was a recipient of the Montana Cowboy Hall of Fame Legacy Award. In 2010, the ranch and barn were again sold and new owners, Tony and Amie James, actively began to reanimate the barn into an event and community center (Figure III.2.4).[9]

In 2015, this spectacular restored barn, which served and thrived through so many changes in use, was nominated and placed on the National Register for Historic Places. Thank you to both Mr. Hamilton and the James family for saving this special barn.

It is hard to resist adding another round barn, located in Three Forks, Montana, that has a similar tiered wedding cake form much like the Doncaster Barn. It is a new structure, purposely built as a venue center for the Headwaters guest ranch established in 2018 (Figure III.2.5).[10] Readers are encouraged to view the photographs on the round barn's website and consider the structural framework of the barn and its interior spaces (Figures III.2.6 and III.2.7).[11]

Figure III.2.6: The unique and expressive structural framing and spacious interior of the Headwaters Ranch Round Barn. Image courtesy of Headwaters Ranch Round Barn.

Figure III.2.7: Interior view of the radial structural patterns, cathedral ceiling, and central skylight. Image courtesy of the Headwaters Ranch Round Barn.

The Headwaters Ranch Round Barn was crafted by its co-owners Kris Nelsen (an artist) and Kevin McCracken (a carpenter and custom furniture designer—Moonlight Furniture). The barn was built with hand-milled, rough-sawn and reclaimed beams. It has a large, spacious environment that can seat some 350 guests.[12]

Its expressive structure and spatial qualities are like a cathedral to round barns and one would be hard-pressed to discern it as a new barn from its historic predecessors.

Three Forks, Montana, is a town with a population of some 2,000 on a high plateau at 4,075 feet above sea level. It sits 30 miles west of Bozeman, home of Montana State University. Three Forks has two unique connections to the greater United States as well as to us. The three forks (or streams) merge and form the headwaters of the Missouri River—the longest river in the country and celebrated by the Missouri Headwaters State Park.[13] The "three forks" were also a point where Lewis and Clark separated to find the best route across the Rocky Mountains to the Pacific Northwest and the Pacific Ocean. Coincidentally, Three Forks is also the original name of Pullman, Washington—the original home of Washington State University as well as our home for forty years. This name "Pullman" is further discussed in the concluding chapter.

Imbrie Round Barn, 1902
Hillsboro, Oregon (currently the Cornelius Pass Roadhouse, Restaurant, Barn, Brewery, and Gardens)

The Imbrie Round Barn has quite an interesting story due to its wide variety of uses over its life. It is currently a venue center for weddings and celebrations (Figures III.3.1 and III.3.2), and it is an important feature of the Cornelius Pass Roadhouse complex and gardens. Although only six acres of the original 1,500-acre Imbrie farm remain, it is a surprisingly delightful historic "rural oasis surrounded by an increasing concentration of freeways, hi-tech office buildings and convenience stores"[14] brought on by suburban sprawl.

Robert Imbrie and his family migrated from the Kingdom of Fife on the southeast coast of Scotland and bought the farm from the original homestead family in the mid-1840s.

The farm is located in Washington County, Oregon, thirteen miles west of Portland.

In the mid-1860s, Robert built a grain shed and replaced the original farmhouse with an elaborate Italian villa-styled home. He also planted a huge grove of English chestnut and black walnut trees; an edible landscape was important to early settlers, as it should be now. Robert and his sons built the 46-foot-diameter octagon barn in 1902; its form is said to be common to their Scottish homeland (Figure III.3.4).[15]

The Imbrie family continued farming in the area until the 1960s. They used the barn for raising workhorses, then as a large dairy barn, and finally for grain, including the famous "Imbrie's barley," a key ingredient in their popular

Blitz-Weinhard beer. The house and farm were placed on the National Register of Historic Places in 1977. That same year, Gary Imbrie (Robert's great-great-great grandson) turned the house into the Imbrie Farmstead Restaurant and in 1984, Donald and Billie Herman purchased the house, barn, and gardens and continued the restaurant that Gary Imbrie had begun (Figures III.3.5–7).[16]

In 1994, the McMenamins took over the restaurant and continued to restore the buildings and property. McMenamins is a unique northwest family company that reanimates historic buildings and properties into venues for handcrafted brew pubs and historic hotels. They now have over 60 locations. The company has done an amazing reanimation and restoration of the Imbrie property, which

Figures III.3.1: The Imbrie octagonal barn in 1982.

The Figures III.3.2: Imbrie octagonal barn in 2018.

includes the historic house, octagon barn, original shed (now a brewery), and a carefully designed and constructed new brew-pub (Figures III.3.8–10) specifically created to suit the historic character preserved throughout the property.[17] (Figure III.3.11)

Figure III.3.3: Aerial view of the six-acre McMenamins' property includes the historic Imbrie house (right of the blue symbol), the new McMenamins' Cornelius Pass Roadhouse Pub, and the octagonal barn (left of the scale symbol). The barn is shaded by 130-year-old English chestnut and black walnut trees. Directly north of the barn is the oldest structure on the property: the original shed, now converted to a brewery. (Google Maps)

Figure III.3.4: The Imbrie-McMenamins' barn today during a celebration. Photo courtesy of Shelley Marie.

Figures III.3.5 and III.3.6: On the left, the intricate framing of the ceiling of the McMenamins' barnt. On the right, the weathervane—a maiden holding the moon and a star.

Figure III.3.7: Interior of the McMenamins' barn.

Figure III.3.8: The Imbrie-McMenamins' "Italian Villa" style house.

Figures III.3.9 and III.3.10: Exterior (left) and interior of the new McMenamins' Cornelius Pass Roadhouse Pub, which was added to the property in the northwestern rustic barn character.

Figure III.3.11: An historic etching of Reedville, a suburb of Hillsboro (three miles from the Imbrie farm). Note a round barn featured in the upper right corner. Whether it was constructed then lost, or only proposed and never built, we don't know, as there is no known record of this barn. Image courtesy of the Oregon Historical Society.

Hyde/Passumpsic Round Barn at the Shelburne Museum, 1909

Shelburne, Vermont

Another successful example of a round barn saved is the Hyde Barn (Figure III.4.1). It was disassembled and moved from East Passumpsic, Vermont, to the Shelburne Museum eighty miles away (Figure III.4.2). It is an 80-foot-diameter structure built in 1901 for Hazen Hyde by Fred "Silo" Quimby,*a contractor who specialized in silo construction. The barn has a Fred Quimby silo in the center for strong central support and for silage to feed the herd below. It is one of approximately two dozen round barns built in the state of Vermont.[18]

Figure III.4.1: The Hyde barn in its original location in East Passumpsic, Vermont. Photo courtesy of the Shelburne Museum.

Figure III.4.2: The Passumpsic Barn in its new location at the Shelburne Museum, Vermont. (Google Maps)

It is an unusual structure in that it has three main floors and was originally built on a hillside to allow direct access to all three levels. The main dairy floor was the second level and accommodated 60 cows. The cows faced inward for feeding, as is typical with round barns. Due to the efficiency of the round barn, the cows could feed in a relatively brief 30 minutes, which then allowed more time for milking, animal care, and other chores. The cows could be milked by the lighted perimeter. The level below was used for storage and clean-up. The manure was removed from the dairy floor through trap doors in the floor, allowing for better sanitation, and it was easily removed to be used

Figure III.4.3: Aerial photo of the former Hyde Barn—now the Passumpsic Barn—in its new and central location at the Shelburne Museum, Vermont. (Google Maps)

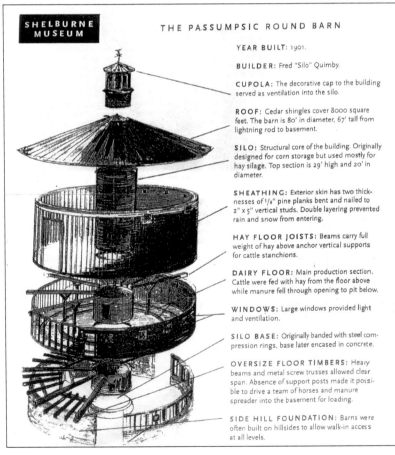

Figures III.4.4 and III.4.5: The Hyde/Passumpsic Barn being reconstructed at the Shelburne Museum site. The image on the left shows the helicopter air-lifting the 9000-pound silo into place. On the right is an illustrated isometric showing the three levels and the various components of this unique barn. Photo and isometric drawing courtesy of the Shelburne Museum.

in the fields. Along with the central silo, the upper floor was used as a loft for storing hay for the dairy herd. It has a central cupola as a fitting crown and provides ventilation. The levels and barn components are effectively illustrated in the drawing in Figure III.4.5.[19]

The Hyde barn was actively used for some 80 years. In 1983, the owner donated it to the Shelburne Museum (Figure III.4.3). After careful analysis by the museum and their architects and engineers, the determination was that it could be disassembled, moved,

and reconstructed at the Shelburne Museum by Graton and Sons, Contractors. The barn components were shipped some 80 miles by truck, but the 9000-pound central silo had to be airlifted across the state by a sky crane helicopter (Figures III.4.4 and III.4.5).[20]

Figures III.4.6, III.4.7, and III.4.8: Top: The beautiful interior of the upper level of the Passumpsic Barn showing the reconstructed roof framing, top of the silo, and cupola above. Photo courtesy of the Shelburne Museum. Bottom left and right: The interior of the lower level of the Passumpsic Barn showing the reconstructed floor framing, new stairs, and new retaining wall. Photo courtesy of the Shelburne Museum; mirror imaged to show both sides of the lower level.

This beautifully restored barn now sits in a central location at the Museum. It serves as a welcome center, a gallery for temporary exhibits, and a venue for civic gatherings (Figures III.4.6 and III.4.7). Its name has changed from the Hyde Family Barn to the Passumpsic Barn. The Shelburne Museum has extensive collections of New England historic buildings, gardens, and some 150,000 artifacts.[21]

A friend returning from a trip to Vermont kindly gave us a postcard of the barn, knowing of our fascination with round barns. We visited the Shelburne Museum website and later called the museum for more information. The museum was very helpful in sending an information sheet and their historian forwarded the photographs we include here. Although we live on opposite sides of the country, hopefully someday we will be able to visit this museum with

its amazing barn. Moving this huge structure demonstrates the myriad possibilities of saving our historic heritage as well as the viability of establishing an outdoor heritage museum in the state of Washington.

*The name Quimby has a very special attachment to us, as it is the rather unusual name we selected for a wonderful family cocker spaniel who lives in our hearts and minds, especially every time we hear that unique name.

Round Barn Restaurant and Banquet Centre, 1912

Champaign, Illinois

The Round Barn Restaurant and Banquet Centre are located in the Round Barn Centre in Champaign, Illinois, named after the round barn on the site (Figures III.5.1–3). The barn was probably built in 1912, soon after the University of Illinois experimental barns in the early 1910s. (Reference pp. 4–6.) In fact, the barn's profile looks the same as the University's first round barn.

Both barns are 60 feet in diameter and originally provided for dairy cows to be housed and fed efficiently around a central silo, with good daylight around the exterior perimeter. The hayloft and access to depositing silage are on the second floor, housed under a massive dome.

Mr. Jatsinas, the current owner of the Round Barn Restaurant and Banquet Centre, stated the barn was moved from its original foundation to its current location, some 200 feet to the southwest, in 1969, as the Health Department would not allow a restaurant to be established with years of "natural fertilizer" embedded in the lower floor. The original foundation remains as a landscape feature, with historic farm equipment displayed in the center (Figures III.5.4 and III.5.5).

Figure III.5.1: The lower level of the round barn and adjacent banqueting center. The white double doors were used for the dairy cows.

The farm and its pastures are now a shopping center and a parking lot. The lower and upper levels of the barn are designed for use as a restaurant (with the silo partially removed). The barn is connected to a building housing a banquet hall with the capacity to serve up to 600 people, one of the largest in east-central Illinois. The Banquet Centre can be divided into two, three, or four separate rooms, allowing for versatility where separate spaces can be created to suit whatever necessity requires for any given function.[22]

As the original barn was not adequately insulated, the heating costs of the massive open space under the dome during cold Illinois winters made it difficult and costly to keep a restaurant open, operating, and profitable. The last time we visited Champaign, the restaurant was closed, but the banquet and catering centers in the adjacent building were still popular. Hopefully, when the roof needs replacement, the owner will insulate more fully prior to installing a new roof so the interiors will be preserved and enjoyed as a restaurant again with improved energy efficiency.

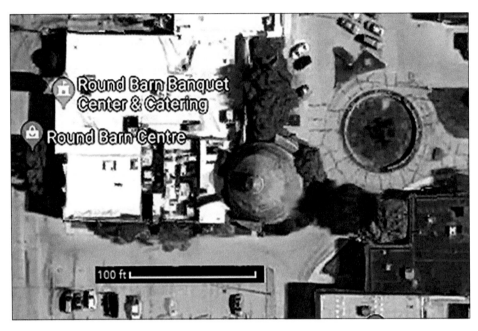

Figure III.5.2: The round barn in the center with the attached banquet and catering center to the left and the original foundation of the barn to the right [Google Maps].

Figure III.5.3: In the foreground, the barn's foundation in its original location, with historic farming equipment displayed in the middle The upper level of the barn restaurant is visible in the background.

Figures III.5.4 and III.5.5: Signs: Round Barn Shopping Centre and Banquet Centre.

We first visited the restaurant as students attending the University of Illinois. When returning for various alumni reunions, we always enjoyed going to this Round Barn Restaurant: it was our favorite. As the illustrations show, the restaurant has an awe-inspiring spatial atmosphere (Figures III.5.6–9). When the architect/designer or contractor removed some of the silo enclosure and created an open lattice-like framework, they created one of the most stunning interiors of any barn we have seen. When combining the truly beautiful, complex, and intricate interior with good food, one can understand why it was always a must-see stop during each return trip. The image showing the interior looking up into the silo and roof is one of our favorite barn photographs (Figure III.5.10). "The Barn Journal" served as the menu and provided interesting information about the barn and its history to all who visited (Figure III.5.11).

Figures III.5.6 and III.5.7: The upper level of the Round Barn Restaurant with the open silo (with numerous boards removed).

Figures III.5.8 and III.5.9: The interior of the ground level. The image on the left is a mirror image of the original image on the right.

Figure III.5.10: The center of the silo looking up to the cupola/skylight and roof framing of the dome. This image is one of our favorite photographs.

Figure III.5.11: "The Barn Journal" and menu produced by the restaurant. It's interesting to note that in 1977, a trip through an extensive salad bar, a ground sirloin burger, and fries cost $3.95 and a cup of coffee cost 40 cents.

Central Wisconsin State Fair Round Barn, 1916

Marshfield, Wisconsin

The Marshfield Barn in Marshfield, Wisconsin, must be included in this publication as it is "the largest round barn in the World"[23] (Figures III.6.1 and III.6.2). Most round barns were proposed to be built between 50 to 90 feet in diameter, which are con-siderable sizes. The Marshfield Barn, however, is an astounding 150 feet in diameter and an impressive 70 feet tall to the top of the crowning cupola (Figure III.6.2). The idea for building such a massive barn was conceived by the Holstein Breeders Association in the early 1900s. It is like a cathedral to agriculture, rivaling some of the world's most iconic buildings (Figures III.6.3 and III.6.4).

This structure was designed and built as a show barn with a huge central arena in 1915–1916 as a prominent

Figure III.6.1: Exterior of the Central Wisconsin State Fair Round Barn. Sign on the upper clerestory walls states the "World's Largest Round Barn"—it is a staggering 150 feet in diameter.[24]

Figure III.6.2: Aerial view of the Central Wisconsin State Fair Round Barn—the largest in the world. (Google Maps)

piece for the Central Wisconsin State Fairgrounds, and it is still used for that primary purpose today. It can house some 250 animals on the ground level and additional smaller animals on the second floor (Figures III.6.5–7). The central area can accommodate approximately 1,000 people, and it is often used for community and social gatherings (Figures III.6.8 and III.6.9).[25]

The barn was designed by William Clark. Like other round barns, the design responded to the agricultural research for efficient dairy practices of the time, enclosing the greatest area with the least surface area (reducing the amount of construction materials required), superior structural stability to storms, and the effectiveness of summer cooling, as warm air rises and is exhausted through the central cupola. Circular buildings also contain the greatest interior floor area with the smallest exterior surface area, thus minimizing heat loss in the winter. In 1915, the $6,000 construction contract was awarded to the seven Felhofer brothers; their bid to construct the barn was some $2,000 less than their nearest competitors, as they had figured out a way to construct the huge dome without internal scaffolding. The roof required some 88,000 individual shingles and was re-roofed several years ago. The barn was originally financed and is now maintained by the Fair

Figures III.6.3, and III.64: Interior of the central space and ceiling showing the beautiful radial structural patterns. At such a height, even the massive timbers used in construction appear as though they are mere toothpicks. Ceiling photo by Josha Harazin 2016.

Figures III.6.5, III.6.6, and III.6.7: Images of the ground level interior of the Marshfield Barn.

Association, the County Board, and private donations, and it is listed on the National Register of Historic Places.[26]

This remarkable barn is by far the largest among approximately one hundred round barns that still stand in the state of Wisconsin.[27] Tours are available to see the barn by contacting the Central Wisconsin State Fair office. Hopefully, the Marshfield Barn will motivate other unique rural structures to find support, function, and even a location to preserve our rural cultural heritage.

Figures III.6.8 and III.6.9: Top, the Marshfield barn exterior during the Central Wisconsin State Fair, and bottom, the interior during a wedding ceremony. Photo by Josha Harazin, 2016.

Round Barn
in 1880 Historic Town, 1919
Midland, South Dakota

T he 1880 Historic Town Round Barn has a uniquely prominent new life—one that we wish other historic structures would find throughout the USA to celebrate and preserve our historic culture and heritage. The historic town site had a modest beginning but, over time, Clarence Hullinger and his son, Richard, developed an extensive collection of historic buildings, including the 60-foot-diameter round barn, railroad trains, and artifacts, which were all moved to the site. It began in 1972 with a gas station that had an old western theme.

About that time, a movie company came to a small town near Midland to film an 1880s-era movie. A main street set was constructed from old buildings and a number of Indian relics and antiques were borrowed from Clarence Hullinger. Winter set in and the filming was abandoned. The movie company returned home giving the main street set to Clarence for the use of his artifacts. The movie set was moved to the 80 acres and the 1880 town was born. The 1880 town came to be through the collecting of buildings, equipment, and contents to recreate an authentic 1880s to 1920s-era town. Clarence and Richard have kept historical value on an equal balance with public appeal, choosing buildings that are not only interesting to look at but which are also historically correct for an early South Dakota town.[29]

The central feature of the development is a fourteen-sided polygon barn, built in 1919 (Figure III.7.1). It houses an extensive museum, a gift shop, and is the entry to the town (Figure III.7.2). The barn was moved to the site from Draper, South Dakota, some 45 miles away. It took three days and thousands of dollars to move this massive structure to its prominent new location (Figure III.7.3 a photo of the move in progress).

Figure III.7.1: Entrance to the 1880s Historic Town and Museum. The entry covering is a carefully crafted addition to the original barn. Note the population of the town: 170 ghosts, 9 cats, 3 dogs and too many rabbits!

Figure III.7.2: An aerial view showing the round barn entry on the left and the extensive collection of historic buildings, equipment, and trains forming the town's main street. At the end of Main Street, opposite the barn, is a beautiful historic church. (Google Maps)

Figure III.7.3: Photo of the barn during its 3-day, 45-mile journey to its new location. This image was taken from a photograph hanging inside the barn.

In the upper story of the barn is a delightful display of original artifacts from the film *Dances with Wolves,* which was filmed near the 1880 town and in nearby Wyoming (Figure III.7.4 and III.7.5). Since it is one of our all-time favorite films, we would like to add that it was adapted from the superb book of the same name written by Michael Blake. As you may remember, the film won seven Academy Awards and is now preserved in the United States Library of Congress Film Registry as "culturally, historically, or aesthetically significant."[30]

Thank you, Clarence and Richard Hullinger, for creating this authentic 1880 town by saving this barn, the historic buildings, trains, and artifacts. They also established an excellent Vanishing Prairie Museum, which houses valuable collections from the General Custer and Buffalo Bill Cody periods, along with extensive Native American artifacts. In the center of the main street is St. Stephan's Church, built in 1915 (Figure III.7.6). It was carefully moved some 120 miles from Dixon, South Dakota, with everything intact, from the stained-glass windows to the bell (which, along with the school and fire bells, may be rung by visitors). The reader is encouraged to visit the town (in person or via its website) to see the extensive collection. The town serves as another example of the ways in which states might develop outdoor museums to display historic and rural town cultural heritage.

Figures III.7.4 and III.7.5: Interior of the upper story of the barn on the left and the original *Dances with Wolves* Native American teepee display on the right. Note both are round with similar structures.

Figure III.7.6: View of the historic main street with its numerous buildings, equipment, and artifacts outside the barn. The church at the far end of Main Street is central.

Kent Dairy Round Barn, 1941
Red Lodge, Carbon County, Montana

The Kent Dairy Barn is quite unique in many ways. It was built as a dairy barn between 1939 and 1941 by the Kent (shortened from the original Kentta) family who settled in Red Lodge in 1917, along with other families from Finland (Figure III.8.1). Their neighborhood was called "Finn Town." The barn was built by Ephraim Kent and his five sons, under the supervision of master barn builder Emery McNamee. The original total investment in the Round Barn in 1941 was approximately $13,000 and the barn is listed on the National Register of Historic Places.[31] It is believed to be the last round dairy barn built in the United States and the only round dairy barn still remaining in the state of Montana. It may also be the only round dairy barn where the ground level walls and part of the upper level wall were constructed with recycled brick, along with timber, and a decorative tin ceiling, salvaged from a building in the neighboring town of Beartooth. The two-story barn is 60 feet in diameter and housed 37 cows on the first level, with a hayloft under its circular dome roof. On the dairy floor, there are twenty-five perimeter windows with an additional twelve windows on the second story. During the summer months, before the hay

Figure III.8.1: Exterior of the Kent Barn in 1989. At that time, it was a restaurant with a community theater and meeting hall on the second level. Note the milk-house extension and the stairs to the second level on the left.

and grain were harvested, the second floor was used for barn dances. The barn also includes a rectangular milk-house extension (Figure III.8.2). Built to accommodate the high mountain climate in Red Lodge, the brick walls are double thickness (13 inches) on the first level and single brick construction above the second floor, and are lined with wood.[32]

Red Lodge is a picturesque town located just outside of the northeast entrance to Yellowstone National Park. The town sits at 5,568 feet in elevation (over a mile high) and offers great skiing in the Rocky Mountains. Close by is Beartooth Pass, one of the highest elevation highway passes in the nation, cresting at over two miles high (10,947 feet). The Beartooth Highway and pass are thought to be among the most beautiful drives in the country. We thought so, too.

When the barn was no longer used as a dairy farm, it fostered many different uses, which other round barn owners might consider. The first time we visited the barn, it had been converted to a restaurant on the lower floor and a delightful community theater on the second, under the dome roof (Figures III.8.3–6). In 2013, the barn was converted into a car dealership and a large repair shop was built immediately adjacent to it, disrupting the original barn setting (Figures III.8.2 and III.8.3). Today the barn is used as a church, rounding out the many uses it has served during its lifetime.

Figure III.8.2: Aerial view of the barn during its current use as a church. Note the large white roof addition, built as an auto service/repair shop when the barn was home to a car dealership. (Google Maps)

Figures III.8.3 and III.8.4: Left, exterior of the barn in 2013 when it was an auto dealership. Right, a welcoming weathervane sculpture above the entrance door reflects the barn's historical past as a dairy farm.

Figure III.8.3: Upper-level structural framing above the theater, 1989.

Figures III.8.4, III.8.5, and III.8.6: Top: Upper-level hayloft converted to a community theatre and meeting hall, 1989. Bottom: Lower level when the barn was used as a restaurant. The photograph on the right is a mirrored image of the original photo on the left. When we visited the barn in 1989, the restaurant was not open yet and the photograph was taken through the window. Note the recycled patterned tin ceiling.

Smith Straw Bale Barn-shaped Round House, 2016

Deary, Idaho

The Smith family home is truly unique as its shape and size are similar to many round barns. Jim Smith carried out extensive research when he and his wife first became interested in building a round straw bale house. They collaborated with Kurt Rathman, then a graduate architectural student at the University of Idaho (UI). UI is located in Moscow, Idaho, just 24 miles from Deary. Kurt had a strong interest in straw bale construction and sustainable design and Jim wanted to build a low-impact house based upon "green" principles.

They built their home in a sunny meadow on picturesque, forested acreage near Deary, Idaho (Figure III.9.1). Deary is a small rural town (population about 500) in the foothills of the Bitterroot Mountains. It is known for its awesome bakery/café in a restored historic building—worth a visit if ever in the region.

Jim acted as the general contractor for the house during construction. He, along with his two sons and various subcontractors, were able to use local materials: straw bales for the walls, structural columns from the timber on the property, and lumber from the surrounding region. This is an important strategy in reducing transportation energy and therefore, global warming. The project was a "labor of love" and took some twelve years to complete.

Figure III.9.1: The Smiths' completed home with straw bale exterior walls.

Kurt Rathman's UI thesis was quite an innovative project. It was a small building demonstrating the various strategies—passive solar, straw bale walls and various uses of recycled materials. It was built adjacent to Moscow's excellent recycling center. Tom often brought his students to the project and had Kurt explain his commitment and the strategies of sustainable design. After graduation and becoming licensed, Kurt established his own firm, emphasizing green issues and straw bale construction. His firm was called "The Three Little Pigs"—but in this case, the houses built from straw bale would not blow down. Straw bale walls are generally 18 inches thick and have double the insulative quality of the best wall construction today (Figure III.9.2). The home was heated by an efficient central "*Envirotect*" radiant masonry heater, like a "Russian" fireplace (Figure III.9.6). The wood used came from their forest and required only a fraction of what a normal fireplace uses (Figures

III.9.3 and III.9.6). As illustrated in Figures III.9.3 and III.9.4, the original plans had a mezzanine surrounding the living area. However, due to convection (where heat automatically rises), they had to install a ceiling for energy efficiency purposes (Figures III.9.6–10). They installed a unique glass panel/skylight in the ceiling so one can still view the beauty in the ceiling structural patterns (Figure III.9.9). Another unique feature often seen in strawbale construction is a "true wall/window," an interior wall 'window' showing the actual strawbales used in construction behind the plaster (Figure III.9.10).

One weekend, Kurt arranged a tour for two of his projects: a straw bale home near Potlatch (18 miles northeast of Moscow) and the Smiths' unfinished round house in Deary (Figures III.9.2 and III.9.3).

In late fall of 2016, Tom received permission to visit the Smiths' completed home with our son, Jon, who helped record the interview. Jim and his

wife, Beverly, were a welcoming couple and gave us a tour explaining various concepts and construction issues while sharing their extensive photo collection. They were quite proud of their family's accomplishments and unique home. The spatial qualities of the house, especially on the second level, were striking and reminiscent of the form and structural patterns of round barns (Figures III.9.3 and III.9.7). Included as well is an amazing round window built into the thick straw bale wall on the stair landing (Figure III.9.11). The Smiths have since passed away and today, reminiscent of Helen King's love for her barn (see pp. 29–30), their final resting place is on the land near their beloved round straw bale house.

Straw bale wall construction was generally known and used in pioneering days and currently in the dry climate of the Southwest. If carefully done, it can effectively be used in the Northwest. Besides the Smith's home,

Figures III.9.2 and III.9.3: The exterior and interior of the Smith home during the field trip led by Kurt Rathman. Note the straw bale construction and the special quality similar to many of the round barns.

Figures III.9.4 and III.9.5: Radial framing of the home. Photos courtesy of Jim Smith from his extensive photo album. Note: to protect the straw bales from getting wet, they had to be installed after the roof was complete.

Figures III.9.6 and III.9.7: Left: Interior of living area with an open kitchen. Right: Interior of second level and gallery.

Figures III.9.8, III.9.9, III.9.10, and III.9.11: The left photo is a view on the Smiths' Envirotect radiant masonry fireplace—note the skylight in the ceiling. The left-middle photograph is a view through the skylight showing the beautiful radiant framing of the roof. The right-middle photo is the "true wall/window" showing the actual straw bale construction alongside of a structural column taken from the timber harvested at the property. The photo on the right is a view through the stunning round window in the thick straw bale wall on the stair landing.

another noteworthy example of straw bale construction is an art studio built in 2001 at IslandWood [IW] a special school in the woods located on Bainbridge Island, Washington (Figure III.9.12). Like the Smith house, IW's art studio is also round, is 50 feet in diameter and has a very efficient wood burning stove in the center—a Tulikivi, one of the most efficient in the world (Figure III.9.13). Straw bale walls have a sculptural quality and effectively accommodate circular/organic forms, beautifully expressed in both Figures III.9.12 and III.9.13.

IslandWood is a unique school created by Debbi Brainerd in 2002. Ms. Brainerd had the will and wisdom to assemble a collaborative team of artists, scientists, educators, students and architects to create this special enterprise. Although commonly referred to as a "school," it is vastly more than

that; it becomes a magical experiential event for all who visit, young and old. The magic of her inspiration raised $52 million in 1998 to develop the programs, purchase the 255-acre site, and complete the campus construction. It has received numerous awards for its unique architecture and innovative programs. IslandWood's buildings were the first in the Pacific Northwest to earn LEED Gold certification (the national green rating system). The Seattle architecture firm, Mithun, was able to integrate Native American characteristics with contemporary and advanced green features. It was initially designed to be a four-day, overnight outdoor experience for fourth to sixth graders. It accomodates 120–160 students per week during the school year. Because of its popularity, it has also become an active conference center and even hosts weddings.[33]

Although most of the 23 buildings at IW are rectangular (the Welcome Center, the Administrative Center, the Dining Hall, the four lodges, Learning Studios, etc.), five of the special Forest Studios are round or polygon shaped. Besides the Art Studio, the Friendship Circle (Figures III.9.14 and III.9.15) and the seven-sided polygon treehouse (Figures III.9.16–19) are a few of the favorites. For the past 20 years, we have been active volunteers at IW. Helen distributes outdoor clothing for the students from its Gear Library and Tom is a docent who leads tours of the Campus. For more information, the reader is encouraged to visit https://sah-archipedia.org/buildings/WA-01-035-0092. For an overview of the programs, campus, and for those interested in IW's sustainable design, visit https://islandwood.org/about-us-an-environmental-science-nonprofit/bainbridge-island-campus/#facilities.

Figure III.9.12: Exterior of Island Wood's Art Studio. Note the thick/sculptural qualities of the straw bale walls. The large entry porch is used for outdoor activities. Photo courtesy of Rob Wagoner.

Figure III.9.13: Interior of IslandWood's Art Studio. Note the Tulikivi wood-burning stove in the center and in the far-left corner is the traditional "truth wall/window" revealing the straw bale wall. Photo courtesy of Rob Wagoner.

Figures III.9.14 and III.9.15: Another special round building at IslandWood is its Friendship Circle. The photo of the Friendship Circle on the left is courtesy of Alison Wowk. The photo on the right shows a group meeting in the Friendship Circle, led by two Native Americans. Both photos edited by Rob Wagoner.

Figures III.9.16 and III.9.17: Top left and right, IslandWood's treehouse overlooks a bog, a unique geological feature. It was designed by Mithun in collaboration with Peter Nelson and Jake Jacobson, who also built the structure.

Figures III.9.18 and III.9.19: Bottom left and right, after much research, the treehouse was carefully attached to a 125-foot-high Douglas fir, ensuring that no damage would come to the tree as a result of the construction.

Notes

1. https://en.wikipedia.org/wiki/Pete_French_Round_Barn

2. https://stateparks.oregon.gov/index.cfm?do=park.profile&parkId=209

3. Beneteau, J. Meadow Ridge Barn Construction Information (personal notes)

4. https://en.wikipedia.org/wiki/Doncaster_Round_Barn

5. https://en.wikipedia.org/wiki/Doncaster_Round_Barn

6. https://en.wikipedia.org/wiki/Spokane, Washington

7. https://en.wikipedia.org/wiki/Spokane_(horse)

8. https://montanacowboyfame.org/inductees/2008/10/the-round-barn-at-twin-bridges

9. https://www.historicroundbarn.com/history

10. https://thevendry.com/venue/80790/headwaters-ranch-three-forks-mt/space/1474

11. https://thevendry.com/venue/80790/headwaters-ranch-three-forks-mt/space/1474

12. https://thevendry.com/venue/80790/headwaters-ranch-three-forks-mt/space/1474

13. https://www.venuereport.com/venue/headwaters-ranch/

14. https://www.waymarking.com/waymarks/WM33YJ_ Cornelius_Pass_Octagonal_Barn_Hillsboro_Oregon

15. https://www.waymarking.com/waymarks/WM33YJ_ Cornelius_Pass_Octagonal_Barn_Hillsboro_Oregon

16. https://www.waymarking.com/waymarks/WM33YJ_ Cornelius_Pass_Octagonal_Barn_Hillsboro_Oregon

17. https://www.mcmenamins.com/

18. "About the Passumpsic Round Barn." Information sheet printed by the Shelburne Museum (Shelburne, Vermont).

19. "About the Passumpsic Round Barn."

20. "About the Passumpsic Round Barn."

21. https://shelburnemuseum.org/collection/round-barn/

22. http://roundbarnbanquetcenter.com/

23. https://www.centralwisconsinstatefair.com/p/other/290

24. https://en.wikipedia.org/wiki/World's_Largest_Round_Barn

25. https://www.centralwisconsinstatefair.com/p/other/290

26. https://www.centralwisconsinstatefair.com/p/other/290, https://en.wikipedia.org/wiki/World's_Largest_Round_Barn

27. https://www.wsaw.com/content/news/Your-Town-Marshfield-Inside-the-Worlds-Largest-Round-Barn-426772231.html

29. https://www.1880town.com/1880-town/history-of-1880-town/, https://en.wikipedia.org/wiki/Dances_with_Wolves

30. https://en.wikipedia.org/wiki/Dances_with_Wolves

31. Kent Dairy Round Barn. National Register of Historic Places Registration: Red Lodge, Carbon County, Montana (Washington, DC: U.S. Department of the Interior, National Park Service, 13 photos from construction through] 1993).

32. Kent Dairy Round Barn. National Register Information System. National Register of Historic Places (Washington, DC: U.S. Department of the Interior, National Park Service, 9 July 2010).

33. https://islandwood.org

Wheat harvest near Othello, in central Washington.

CHAPTER IV

Reanimating Barns, Buildings, and Rural Communities

Perhaps Black Elk explained it best:

Everything the power of the world does is done in a circle. The sky is round, and I have been told that the earth is round…The wind in its greatest power whirls. Birds make nests in circles…Our teepees are round…and these were always set in a circle, the nation's hoop, a nest of many nests…

Proactive community involvement is a critical factor when trying to save historic barns and buildings, whether on rural farms or in towns. Such change takes time for effective collaborative leadership and community citizen-based organizations to succeed—and it takes people with the will and wisdom to save our historic heritage to lead the way to a sustainable future. The very act of participating in preservation teaches important lessons, vital for future generations to understand.

We inventoried the round barns of Washington state in Chapter II. We visited other round barns in locations across the country to explore potential alternative uses to demonstrate how these unique structures can be saved in Chapter III. In Chapter IV, we look at community-based preservation projects and citizen involvement—how these combined efforts can save our historic cultural heritage and promote sustainability and stronger communities at the same time.

Throughout this book, we emphasize the importance of fostering community and state involvement to support efforts in saving these disappearing structures. Both the Washington State Department of Archaeology and Historic Preservation (DAHP, https://dahp.wa.gov) and the statewide nonprofit Washington Trust for Historic Preservation (https://preservewa.org) offer vital guidance and potential resources. These organizations can provide leadership, funding, and technical assistance on most historic rehabilitation projects located within the state of Washington. Other states offer their own historic preservation organizations that can provide similar assistance. The National Trust for Historic Preservation has field operations across the country at which their staff focus on place-based preservation and local, state, and federal advocacy for preservation-friendly policies. They work closely with an ever-growing network of statewide and local partner organizations and with local preservationists nationwide. The main headquarters are in Washington, DC, and inquiries can be directed to info@savingplaces.org. These resources can prove invaluable to any preservation project, most particularly in the preliminary planning stages. Just being aware that help is available can provide emotional support to carry on, when a small dose of courage can be helpful to address daunting tasks. Tackling such projects is best not left to the faint of heart.

In Chapter III, we visited and explored a select number of barns that were reanimated in different ways to serve new purposes. In some cases, the barns were moved to new locations to fulfill their destiny in a sustainable future. All represent a diversity of ideas, creative uses that will continue to support their surrounding communities well into the future, and whose original ideas could be borrowed and adapted to suit other locations. In this chapter, we discuss two very special rectangular barns that have been saved and reanimated into unique ways that greatly enhance their communities.

Since barns, buildings, and people group together to create communities, we will end this chapter with stories of saving important historic buildings to reanimate the "rural" town/city where we lived for 40 years—Pullman, Washington, home to the flagship campus of Washington State University. Pullman has two distinct personalities: during the summer, with most university students absent, it is a small, quiet, rural town; and during the school year, when the students return, it is a vibrant city. It is important to remember that the word "city" is derived from "civility," a foundation to our civilization.

We grew up in a semi-urban community west of Chicago and loved the diversity and culture of the city. When we arrived in Pullman in 1963, we were surprised (maybe shocked) at its small size and rural character. Over the years, we fell in love with its friendly culture and historic qualities, surrounded by the stunning Palouse landscape and the beautiful Northwest. Pullman was a wonderful place to raise our family and practice our skills at collaborative learning as educators.

Consequently, this chapter focuses on citizen involvement in saving and reanimating not only barns but also buildings and a sense of community. This is an important story to conclude this book. The community-based participation and initiatives were, for the most part, successful. Although change takes time, those with the patience and perseverance to follow through were indeed inspiring. Here, we attempt to reconstruct past activities in saving not only Pullman's historic heritage, but also reanimating its inherited natural qualities. Pullman's story, and that of its citizenry, can offer insight into creating a brighter, more profound, and sustainable future for all communities and our planet.

Washington State University's Historic Barn Restoration into an Alumni Centre

Pullman, Washington

●

Washington State University's historic barn is not a round barn but rather a rectangular U-shaped barn. Its story may add some inspiration for saving other important structures. WSU's huge cattle barn was constructed in 1922. It was designed by Rudolph Weaver, who served as the campus architect from 1911 to 1923. He designed six other prominent buildings on campus including the President's House (now the Ida Lou Anderson House), Carpenter Hall, and four residence halls. Weaver also established and was the first chair of WSU's architecture department.[1]

The barn is a U-shaped two-story structure with two prominent silos on the west side (Figures IV.1.1 and

Figure IV.1.1: Photograph of the west elevation of the WSU barn in 1925. The hayloft access is on the left side of the barn. Courtesy of WSU Photographic Archives.

Figure IV.1.2: The reanimated west elevation of the barn, now WSU's Lewis Alumni Centre, as of 1989. What appear to be silos are actually imitating the original historic structures and currently serve as public restrooms. The historic Victory Bell is front and center in the entry plaza along with the flag poles.

Figure IV.1.3: Historic photograph of the east elevation of the WSU barn in 1922. Courtesy of WSU Photographic Archives.

IV.1.2). The cattle were grazed and housed on the ground level and the huge second level hayloft was serviced by a ground-level bridge on the north side. The barn was also an important symbol of WSU's early years as the state's only land-grant institution and its international leadership in agriculture, veterinary science, and animal care. The barn was saved and reanimated into WSU's Lewis Alumni Centre in 1989 (Figure IV.1.3 and IV.1.4). There are many fun tales about how this magnificent barn was saved. But equally important and vitally critical are the lesser-known stories about the faculty and architecture students' creativity and influence that may have helped saved it from demolition.

Thousands of alumni and friends of WSU across the country rallied around the project with donations of building materials and funds for construction. WSU alumni Steve McNutt and Robert "Bob" Grossman, architects at the Northwest Architectural Company in the Seattle area, designed the "new" building. Over several years the renovations were completed and, on March 31, 1989, the Lewis Alumni Centre was officially dedicated and presented to the University as a gift from WSU's alumni and friends. The Centre is a true gem on campus, often referred to as the "living room of the campus."[2]

The WSU Lewis Alumni Centre is indeed a treasure: a grand living room to welcome alumni and visitors to the Pullman campus. It is a symbol of WSU's heritage and a wonderful achievement in saving and restoring a significant historic barn.

Figure IV.1.4: The reanimated east elevation of the barn, now WSU's Lewis Alumni Centre, 2015.

In addition to the successful reanimation of the barn, the architects designed two entry plazas. The east entry opens to guest parking and a welcoming courtyard nestled between the two projecting sides of the U-shaped barn (Figures IV.1.4 and IV.1.5). The west entry, facing the main campus, is a gathering plaza and home to the historic 1892 Victory Bell (Figures IV.1.5 and IV.1.6).

Starting in 1892, the bell tolled to signal the beginning of classes. Then, in 1930, it was moved onto the roof of College Hall, to be rung following football victories. In 1998, it was installed at its current location, the west plaza overlooking the main campus, and it is still used to celebrate Cougar football wins.[3]

The architecture department's involvement in the restoration and redevelopment of the cattle barn into an alumni center began one afternoon in the early 1980s when one of WSU's architecture students, who worked parttime for the University, came into Tom's office and discreetly stated he was to process a demolition order to remove the historic barn from its much-desired campus location. WSU was landlocked on three sides by urban growth and the only available (and much-coveted) land was to the east, where the barn was located. As a student, Jim Weddell was very interested in historic preservation and was among the first of many to complete a research paper on the round barns of the Palouse.

Jim told Tom that he had put the demolition assignment at the bottom of his stack of work orders. Both men were quite concerned about the removal of such a significant historic barn, and they decided to check it out to see if it was worthy of saving. Three other colleagues were also interested in the barn: Henry Matthews, an architectural historian, and Noel and Alina Moffet, visiting design professors. All three were from England and had considerable experience in historic conservation as well as historic building restoration.

Henry had reanimated a sixteenth-century forge, which he and his wife carefully converted into their home. Now professor emeritus, Henry had written numerous books on the Northwest and European/Asian architectural history. Noel and Alina were both architects and educators doing restoration work in England and Poland. Their personal enthusiasm and creativity in architecture and life enriched ours and all they touched.

Upon visiting the cattle barn, we were amazed at the grandeur and quality of the structure. The upper story and its gambrel roof trusses created a massive, awe-inspiring space, as beautiful as any space on campus—likened to a cathedral dedicated to agriculture (Figures IV.1.7–10). Tom remembers with great delight Henry's method of testing for structural decay: his instrument was nothing more than a small pocketknife that he would push into various structural members; fortunately, no significant decay was found.

The architecture professors decided to do a design studio project with some forty-five students on ways to restore and reuse the barn. Henry gave a presentation on the preservation of rural buildings in England; Tom presented on the history of round barns on the Palouse and included adaptive strategies of other barns discussed in this work (museums, demonstration farms, restaurants, etc.). They obtained approval to revisit the barn with the students, who were equally inspired by the majesty and beauty of the structure and the challenges of finding an appropriate reuse for it on campus. They generated many original and creative ways in which the barn could be reused. Some proposed a museum on the history of WSU and its advancements in science and agriculture; others designed a student activity center, a campus-wide conference center, and even a restaurant with demonstration gardens specializing in Palouse-grown produce. As the location was close to the football stadium, others proposed it as an alumni center, which would be a special place to welcome past graduates. A few students proposed a program to sell tiles to all alumni to help pay for the barn's restoration—a strategy later adopted by the university to do just that. The results of the students' creativity were posted in the Student Union Gallery on campus. The *Daily Evergreen*, the student newspaper, also printed an article on the exhibition.

Henry was chair of the WSU historic preservation committee and Tom chaired the university planning committee. Both discussed the barn with their colleagues and encouraged its preservation and reuse. Soon thereafter, Samuel Smith, the university president at the time, and Keith Lincoln, one of WSU's great football players and then director of the alumni association, proposed converting the barn into a new Alumni Centre. We like to think the student and faculty efforts, along with their original and creative ideas, influenced this decision. The concept took hold, and President Smith and Keith were successful in their fundraising efforts to reanimate the barn into the truly amazing Alumni Centre and meeting place for related campus activities that it has become.

After graduating from the WSU architecture program, Jim Weddell became the director of Pullman's Main Street Program (MSP), effectively reanimating the historic character of downtown Pullman and many other local buildings (including the Wagon-Wheel Barn and Artisan Center in Uniontown, WA, discussed later).

After their years at WSU, Henry, Noel, and Alina were an integral part of Tom's teaching and research in England. Tom's favorite "classrooms" were the streets of London, with its historic and contemporary developments, and England and Scotland's stunning historic towns and cities. Tom was fortunate to have directed five semester-long programs based in London. Noel, as past president of London's Architectural Association (AA), was instrumental in arranging for WSU's program to be housed there. The AA is the oldest (and some say the best) architectural program in the world. It was established by and continues to be governed by the users—the students.

During Tom's year-long sabbatical in 1979–80, Henry helped us find a sixteenth-century townhouse in Hatfield Broad Oak, a picturesque medieval village outside of London. It was here that he lived in a beautifully restored "Old Forge"—reanimated and restored by Henry and his family (Figures IV.1.11–13). Along with many historic buildings, this picturesque medieval village boasts a sixteenth-century tithe barn[4] that had been gracefully converted into three townhouses (Figures IV.1.14–6).

As mentioned previously, Professor Weaver, the architect who originally designed WSU's cattle barn, also designed Carpenter Hall, which housed the architecture department and was home base for Tom's architectural teaching (and our research into the round barns) for forty years. Tom, along with others in the department, had a strong interest in the historic preservation of buildings and districts and helped create a design studio module for students' senior year on evaluating and reanimating historic buildings and districts. He became coordinator of that project and was always in search of actual buildings and real design projects for the students' creative and professional development. Many of the stories presented in this section were an integral part of that design studio module and were enriched by the students' enthusiasm, originality, creativity, and designs. Tom and his colleagues actually proposed reanimating Carpenter Hall as a studio design project, with the goal of housing all the design disciplines at WSU (interior design, architecture, landscape architecture, and regional planning) in one building. It seems this was a rather challenging and popular project which was repeated every four to five years. It

Figure IV.1.5: Aerial view of the WSU historic barn reanimated into an Alumni Centre. The main campus is west (left) of the center. The trees open outward towards the campus to welcome visitors and an entry plaza includes an historic Victory Bell, which is rung when the WSU Cougars win home football games.

Figure IV.1.6: The 1892 Victory Bell on the west plaza of the Alumni Centre, overlooking the main campus.

Figures IV.1.7 and IV.1.8: Above, the original second-level hayloft in 1983 (photo courtesy of Henry Matthews) and below, the reanimated loft in 2015.

Figures IV.1.9 and IV.1.10: On the left, the original first-level as it looked in 1983 (photo courtesy of Henry Matthews) and on the right the reanimated ground level in 2015.

is interesting to note that the "Design Disciplines" concept was proposed for decades without resolution, while numerous new building projects were proposed at various times throughout the campus. Finally, in the 1980s, it was resolved that Carpenter Hall should be remodeled and expanded as the home of the School of Architecture and Construction Management. The remodeling was completed in 1985 but it took until 2011 for the design disciplines to coalesce and integrate into the School of Design and Construction. Today, Carpenter Hall is home to all design disciplines at WSU.

WSU, as a prominent land-grant university for over 125 years, has had numerous agricultural structures, many of which have disappeared over time. It is quite fortunate that the historic cattle barn was saved and converted into the Alumni Centre we have today.

In their historical archives, the university houses an extensive collection that addresses all manner of WSU buildings, agricultural structures, and the round barns in the Palouse region that were documented in Chapter II. Most recently, as we explored a Pullman Centennial publication,[5] we discovered a photograph that raised the possibility of a round barn having existed on WSU's campus (Figure IV.1.17).

Amazed, we had not seen it during many research sessions over the years and we were delighted at the prospect of a round barn on campus. The agriculture faculty at the time would have known of research from other land-grant universities on the efficiency of round barns and might have built one on WSU's campus.

With the help of Mark O'English of WSU's Manuscripts, Archives, and Special Collections (MASC), we learned that the structure in the photo that appeared to be a round barn was,

in fact, the south elevation of an elongated oval cattle pavilion built in 1904 (Figure IV.1.18). Unfortunately, the pavilion had long since been removed and the U-shaped barn to the right of the pavilion (shown in Figures IV.1.17 and IV.1.18) was destroyed by a fire in the 1930s. The U-shaped barn was similar to but was actually much smaller than the cattle barn reanimated into the Alumni Centre. We were disappointed that we had not found another round barn—especially one on WSU's campus.

Figures IV.1.11, IV.1.12, and IV.1.13: Hatfield Broad Oak and the Matthews' home, a restored sixteenth-century blacksmith's forge.

Figures IV.1.14, IV.1.15, and IV.1.16: Restored Tithe Barn reanimated into three townhomes in Hatfield Broad Oak, England.

Figure IV.1.17: Above, the structure left of the U-shaped barn appears to be a round barn on WSU's campus. Courtesy of WSU Historic Archives.
Figure IV.1.18: In the lower image, seen from a different angle, it is clear that the structure was an elongated cattle pavilion with round ends (i.e., oval) on WSU's campus. Courtesy of WSU Historic Archives.

Dahmen Wagon-Wheel Barn Reanimated into Artisans Center

Uniontown, Washington

The Dahmen Wagon-Wheel Barn in Uniontown, Washington, is named after its striking and distinctive fence, built from over one thousand metal wheels and gears, composed and welded together by Steve Dahmen. Even the weathervane atop the barn features a wheel (Figures IV.2.1–4). Uniontown, a small agricultural community of approximately 350 residences, is located 17 miles south of Pullman. The fence is known throughout the Palouse region, and likely farther afield. It has been featured in *National Geographic* magazine, and one visitor even reported she saw a photograph of it hanging in a restaurant in China.[6]

The barn was originally constructed in 1935 by Frank Wolf, to serve as a dairy barn for the Jack Dahmen family. They continued the dairy farm until 1953 when the property and barn were purchased by Steve and Junette Dahmen, both of whom were accomplished artists. Steve constructed the wagon-wheel fence over a thirty-year period, and it has become a delightful landmark of the site. Steve stated that every wheel—many of which were donated by neighbors—has a unique history with its own story.

In 2004, Steve and Junette donated the barn to the Uniontown Community Development Association (UCDA), a non-profit organization. After much community involvement,

the UCDA decided that this barn, with its wagon-wheel fence, should be reanimated into an art center. Jim Weddell, the architecture student who helped save the WSU Cattle Barn, worked for Whitman County Community Development at that time and was

instrumental in the whole process—in fostering community involvement, and in helping UCDA President Dale Miller apply for and obtain grants for the extensive renovation. Jim stated that one of the most challenging issues was stabilizing the structure.

Figure IV.2.1: The Dahmen wagon-wheel fence and barn. The shed on the right was removed and the wood saved and reused. A new building with similar character and form now sits in its place.

Figures IV.2.2, IV.2.3, and IV.2.4: Steve Dahmen's design of the thousand-plus wheels and gears in the wagon-wheel fence and weathervane on the top of the barn.

Figure IV.2.5: Interior of the barn showing the upper level of the Artisans Center. Note the L-shaped mezzanine on the upper left and rear of photo, which is currently used to display artwork for sale. The artists' studios are located behind sliding glass doors on this level, with additional studios on the main level.

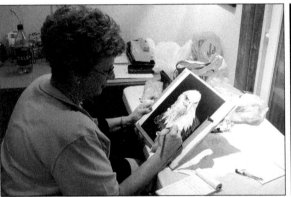 

Figures IV.2.6 and IV.2.7: On the left, artist Judy Fairley works on a beautiful scratchboard etching of a bald eagle; and the finished product on the right, which we purchased.

Figure IV.2.8: The Dahmen Barn with the new addition on the right.[11]

He found Fearless Engineering in Missoula, Montana, which developed methods to straighten and stabilize the barn. Their cross-bracing system is considered an engineering work of art. A local contractor, Marv Entel of RESSCO, did the reconstruction with the extensive aid of community volunteers: "This was truly a labor of love by the community for this old barn."[7] An elevator and restrooms were added to the back of the barn, so, when viewed from the highway, the barn has retained its original form.[8] In 2006, the grand opening of the Artisans Center was held, with much fanfare throughout the community (Figure IV.2.5–7).

By 2011, the demand for artists' studio space exceeded the barn's capacity, and plans were begun for an addition. Hutchison and Maul, architects from Seattle, volunteered their time to work with UCDA and the community to select an option for expansion. The selected scheme replaced the old loafing shed with a new structure modeled after the original historic form. The contractor and community members volunteered their time to dismantle the shed, carefully saving the wood siding to be reused on the new addition. The new loafing shed allows the Center to flourish and includes a display of agricultural life of the surrounding Palouse region (Figure IV.2.8).[9] The Dahmen Barn Artisans Center maintains a website for observing community events and activities that are all part and parcel of this creative barn's exciting venture.[10]

Thank you all for reanimating this barn, enriching the arts both locally and throughout the Palouse region, and for demonstrating the many ways to preserve our historic agricultural heritage and rural culture.

Nick's Barn Restaurants
Elgin, Illinois

Nick Sarillo has developed a special way of saving the extensive resources embodied in historic barns: he recycles and reuses them in constructing his uniquely "new and old" restaurants in Illinois. His first location was built in Crystal Lake in 1995 (Figure IV.3.1) and the second in Elgin in 2005. Although this process does not save the actual barns, it does preserve the original handcrafted construction and timber resources. After he purchases the barns, which are generally about to collapse or be torn down, he then dismantles them and reuses the heavy timber trusses, the irreplaceable handcrafted joinery, and time/weather-enriched siding to shape and construct his popular Pizza & Pub restaurants. (A virtual tour of the Crystal Lake restaurant can be seen at https://nickspizzapub.com.)

Before building his first restaurant, Nick spent twelve years in the construction business. During that time, he developed effective experience for building his individual restaurants—where to save and where to go for the best materials. He wanted to build a large barn-like restaurant (8,300 square feet) with an unforgettable intimate atmosphere. He insisted on using recycled old barn timbers and wood. Fortunately, he was able to rescue a historic barn from Marengo, Illinois, sixteen miles west of Crystal Lake. The owner of the old barn was so happy that someone would remove the dilapidated barn that he offered it to Nick free of charge. Nick, along with his brother, an architect, designed the restaurant with the old barn materials and coordinated the construction. They made sure the timber and wood

were safe and insect-free by putting everything through a dry kiln. He also constructed the restaurant in the manner of a traditional barn-raising, having his family and friends in the building trades participate. It must have been quite an amazing process.[12]

Nick Sarillo is a very creative and innovative restaurant owner and his success has extended to being an author, educator, and speaker with a deep concern for our planet. He states:

> In the last decade, "green" has gone mainstream. This is good news not only for the planet, but also for business. Consumers want to make more sustainable lifestyle choices—whether it's for hybrid cars, non-toxic cleaning supplies, or organic groceries. By serving this growing market, smart, forward-thinking businesses are innovating ways to grow and make a

Figure IV.3.1: Exterior of Nick's Pizza & Pub restaurant in Crystal Lake, Illinois.

Figures IV.3.2 and IV.3.3: Interior of Nick's Pizza & Pub restaurant in Elgin, Illinois.

profit *while* contributing to solving our world's big challenges.

For us, "sustainability" means more than our stewardship of natural resources. We take the sustainability of our human resources just as seriously. In fact, our concept of sustainability includes both external-focused practices, such as recycling, and internal, human practices, such as personal development training. By combining an exterior/ natural and an interior/human focus, we arrive at an integrated—or "integral" (meaning balanced and whole)—concept of sustainability.

While conventional sustainability aims to improve the health of the environment, our "integral sustainability" also addresses the mental, emotional, and spiritual health of our workplace and team members...Thus, as we're helping sustain our planet, we're also sustaining our people. And it's setting us apart from our competition in a serious way.[13]

Nick's creative approach is a huge recycling effort, which helps our

planet in at least five important ways. First, it saves the extensive materials and new trees that would be needed to supply the huge timbers and cut lumber to construct a new structure for the restaurant. Second, it saves trees that can still breathe in carbon dioxide (CO_2) from the atmosphere, exhaling oxygen and converting the CO_2 into more carbon-based fiber (wood). Third, if the old barns were not recycled, they would

become rural ruins. As wood decays, it releases stored CO_2 back into the atmosphere from its carbon fibers. Recycling the wood prevents a huge amount of CO_2 from being released, much more than if this pile of wood were simply burned, causing a rapid release of CO_2 back into the air. Fourth, if barn wood is harvested from nearby regions, it saves the enormous amount of energy used to cut down new trees; ship, process,

Figures IV.3.4 and IV.3.5: Antique wooden wagon wheel and custom light fixture made from antlers.

Figures IV.3.6 and IV.3.7: The round barn was a few miles northwest of Elgin, Illinois. At one time, it was proposed as an agriculture education center, but it has since disappeared. The pond and fountain were for a new office park complex (a reservoir for cooling the new complex).

and manufacture the wood into new lumber products; and then ship the wood long distances from the mills to the construction sites. And lastly, it allows the public to appreciate the qualities of historic barn construction while enjoying Nick's creativity in both recycling and in the kitchen.

As discussed earlier, we grew up in Illinois and have family still living in the area, including Downers Grove, Elgin, Pontiac, and other nearby regions. When we visit, we enjoy meeting together at one of Nick's restaurants and appreciate its unique "barn" atmosphere, its collection of antiques (another recycling process), and his delicious food (Figures IV.3.2–5). We always order Nick's special pizza, both regular and gluten-free. Thank you, Nick Sarillo.

Coincidentally, just a few miles away from Nick's was a majestic round barn with a good, solid intact roof (Figures IV.3.6 and IV.3.7). The community tried to save it during the time Nick was building his restaurant. The barn would have made an engaging center for agricultural education but, unfortunately, the last time we visited Elgin, it had sadly disappeared due to suburban expansion and sprawl. We wonder what Nick could have created from its beautiful form and structural qualities.

Moving and Reanimating a Historic Barn

Pullman, Washington

In 1994, a group of Pullman citizens interested in reanimating old barns discussed moving a historic barn to Pullman. The group, part of the Greystone Foundation, was led by Robert (Bob) Wayne, who was a new optometrist in Pullman. Bob had a love for historic barns and prior experience in historical construction methods. He proposed rescuing, moving, and re-erecting an old barn to a location adjacent to the community gardens on a large plot of land on the historic Koppel farm, near downtown and the university. He even had an offer of a barn: the huge historic Higby barn owned by the Clark family (Figures IV.4.1 and IV.4.2).

The way that our mutual barn interests intersected is a special story. We asked Bob and his wife Leslie how and why they moved from Texas to Pullman. He said they were visiting a friend in Colfax and decided to explore the picturesque Palouse region and its neighboring towns. They approached Pullman from Colfax and as they arrived, cresting the final, golden, wheat-covered Palouse hills, they saw Pullman's townscape set in a striking green valley filled with trees, the university, and Moscow Mountain in the background. They were so delighted with the scene before them that they said, "we need to move here!" (Figure IV.4.3). They did make Pullman their home, set up their optometrist practice, and waited for their first clients. They waited and waited and waited...finally, they sadly concluded that this move wasn't going to work out. In a make-or-break moment, they decided to wait one more week, and fortunately, their office phone finally started to ring, thereby making their optometry services a success after all. We were one of those who called and appreciated their professional services. On Tom's first visit, we discovered our mutual interest in historic barns.

To advance the project and the moving of the Higby/Clark barn, Bob began a "fun and fund-raiser" for the project. He also asked Jack Sobon, a friend who was also an architect, author, and national expert on traditional timber frame construction from Windsor, Maine, to come to Pullman and conduct a multi-day workshop to demonstrate and train interested people on how to construct or reconstruct barns (Figures IV.4.4–6).[14] Jack uses authentic, historic handcrafted tools exclusively for his projects. Bob was able to secure rough-cut timber used in historic barn construction for this project. The three-day workshop ended with the construction of a small barn, now used as a tool storage building for the community gardens.

Figures IV.4.1 and IV.4.2: The Clark historic barn with Bob Wayne and a group of WSU architecture students studying the barn.

Figure IV.4.3: Picturesque view of Pullman and WSU with the campus clock tower as the highest feature.

The barn group envisioned moving the Higby/Clark barn and creating a special place for community events along with a farmer's market. Tom got approval to offer a special elective course in architecture, and those students created measured drawings of the existing barn, preliminary construction drawings, and scale models to convert it into a community market and center that met current city and building codes (Figures IV.4.7–10). John Benedict, an architectural computer-aided design and drafting (CADD) expert, did final digital construction drawings for the conversion. Also, Robert Hoyle, a civil engineer, volunteered to do an extensive structural analysis of the barn for its new use and location. The plans with the structural analysis were approved by the city and we were ready to have barn builder Jack Sobon return and direct the process.

Our dream was about to become a reality. Unfortunately, after budget and liability issues were carefully considered, we realized that the project

Figures IV.4.4 and IV.4.5: The barn community workshop. On the left, Jack Sobon is demonstrating a drilling machine and, on the right, is on top center of the completed framing for the handcrafted shed. Bob Wayne is the second from the left on the lower level and Tom was behind the camera taking the picture.

Figures IV.4.6: The completed shed and the market tent where the barn was proposed, with the community gardens and university in the background.

was far beyond our current capacity at that time. We all decided to take some time off to reevaluate and hope in the future it would become a reality—and we are still waiting. The community gardens established an active farmer's market at the time, but it was housed in a large tent rather than in a barn. Without the additional support of the entire barn project, the farmer's market was temporary and is not currently operational.

Figures IV.4.7, IV.4.8, IV.4.9 and IV.4.10: The upper images show the students' model with and without the roof. The lower left shows the model interior; the lower right, a CAD drawing by John Benedict.

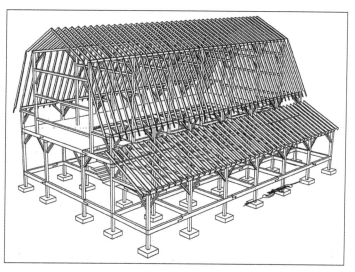

Saving Historic Buildings and Rural Communities

Since we spent forty years in Pullman, we thought it would be interesting to highlight other community attempts to enhance and preserve the region's historic, cultural, and environmental qualities—all important to foster civility and enhance a deepening sense of community. The following examples are not barns, but they are sigificant structures that highlight the critical importance of citizen involvement and initiatives. From a day-to-day perspective, these attempts seem painfully slow, but looking back, there is a record of many wonderful achievements. We hope that these successful efforts may offer considerable encouragement to other individuals and communities. The underlying principles within all these stories are proactive involvement and collaboration, organizing into supportive groups, being positive, persevering, and having patience. Change can take a lot of time.[15]

Greystone Foundation and the Greystone Church

The Greystone Foundation was originally a citizen-based non-profit non-governmental organization (NGO) created to save the historic Greystone Church in Pullman. The Greystone Church was built in 1898 by the United Presbyterian Church. The architect William Swain was a self-taught immigrant from England who moved to Pullman in

Figures IV.5.1 and IV.5.2: Exterior of the Greystone Church on the left. On the right, view from the balcony showing the beautifully crafted wood and steel ceiling trusses. Photos courtesy of Henry Matthews.

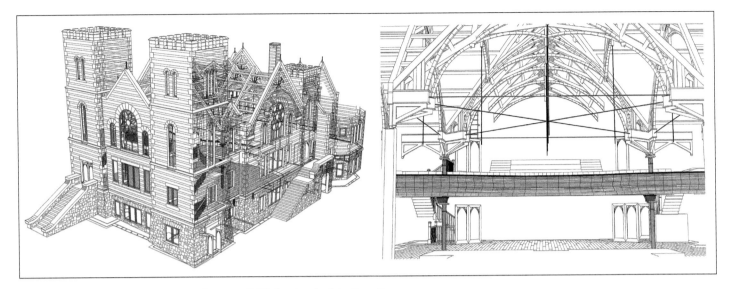

Figures IV.5.3 and IV.5.4: Exterior and interior CAD drawings by John Benedict.

1891. The building is a magnificent Neo-Romanesque building (Figure IV.5.1). Its exterior is made up primarily of basalt stone found in the region. Its interior has stunning wood trusses with steel tension rods and a carefully crafted wood interior with elegant stained-glass windows (Figure IV.5.2–7). It is clearly equivalent to the most impressive historic churches, even those in Europe.

In 1963, the Presbyterian church moved to a new location and sold the building to the Spokane Diocese of the Roman Catholic Church. It was renamed the St. Thomas More Chapel and was used as a student center from 1964 to 1980. However, during the 1980s it sat vacant.[16] The Greystone Foundation, then led by realtor Dick Domey, tried for many years to save it by finding a new

owner. The property, close to WSU's campus, was quite valuable despite the fact that the building continued to deteriorate. Tom and fellow colleagues teamed up to conduct multiple design studies with WSU's landscape architecture, architecture, and interior design students. The students thought the building would make an ideal community/cultural center, theater/restaurant, and/or

Figures IV.5.5, IV.5.6, and IV.5.7: On the left and center are some of the stunning stained-glass windows. On the right is another stained-glass window found in one of the spacious apartments. Photos courtesy of Glenn and Melodie Petry Papers; Manuscripts, Archives, and Special Collections; Washington State University Libraries.

museum as well as functioning as a church. The Greystone Foundation was successful in placing the church on the National Historic Register, and the group had numerous meetings with the university and the city of Pullman about saving it. In 1998, the foundation held a huge open house to celebrate the church's 100-year anniversary. Donations helped repair some of the most critical problems (primarily the roof) and placed exterior glass coverings to protect the fragile stained-glass windows (Figures IV.5.5–7). We all loved the building, but no one had come forward to purchase it or reanimate it into a church or another adaptive use.

Fortunately, in 2004 Glenn Petry, a retired professor of finance, and his wife Melodie bought the building, in hopes of restoring it into a coffee house, theater, and museum. After considerable study, the Petrys found a creative way to save and restore the building, converting it into fourteen apartments. Later, they donated the building to the College Hill Association, and it continues to serve as a local rental housing option.

Gladish High School

The Gladish High School is another elegant historic building that was almost destroyed. Named for Oscar Gladish, a beloved high school principal and longtime mayor of Pullman, the Gladish structure is a massive building complex in a central location, near to and overlooking Pullman's downtown with a distant view of the University (Figure IV.5.8). Gladish served as Pullman High School from 1925 to 1972. It is important for us to emphasize that schools should be an integral part of our neighborhoods and communities.

Pullman is shaped like a four-leaf clover, having four neighborhoods on four distinct hills joined by the downtown "center" along with three forks of the rivers and streams in the valley. The hills are Pioneer Hill (where the original settlers lived and farmed), College Hill (where the university and much of the student housing are located), Military Hill (where there once was an academy, long since gone) and Sunnyside Hill (which gets sun throughout the day). It is always intriguing to trace the meanings behind the names of places.

The Pullman school board proposed a new high school on the far north edge of town and, despite being heavily contested, the bond issue passed by a slim margin. Pullman's middle school was on the far south side of the town. The opponents argued that, instead of a new high school, a middle school should be built on the north side, to balance the community and allow more students to walk or bike to their schools. Drawing on well-established community planning principles, Tom, along with Pollard and Darlene Dickson

Figures IV.5.8 and IV.5.9: Exterior and interior of the auditorium of the Gladish Community and Cultural Center.

and colleagues in the architecture department, challenged the idea of building a high school on the edge of town. Pollard Dickson was a mature and gifted architecture student who later went on to save and move the rural town of North Bonneville, WA.

The new high school, along with a large parking lot, was built on the north edge of town, on some of the finest agricultural land in the country. Most students could no longer walk to their middle or high schools or be part of the downtown community. Most now had to take a bus, have parents drive them, or, if they were old enough and could afford a car, drive to school: more cars, more sprawl, more energy consumed, causing more CO_2 to be pumped into the atmosphere and more global warming.

Gladish was subsequently used for offices and private schools, but the building was poorly maintained. In the early 1990s, the school district decided to sell the historic building. When the school district accepted an offer from a developer planning to raze the complex to build more housing, another citizens' group, the Friends of Gladish (FOG), was formed to save the historic building complex. FOG challenged the sale on the grounds that it was not properly advertised and opened to other offers. The school board had to re-advertise the sale and the Friends of Gladish developed an investment plan. We, along with many local citizens, invested in the project in the hopes of saving it. Fortunately, FOG was able to outbid the developer and bought the historic building. Beverly McConnell, president with the FOG Board, dedicated an abundance of time and resources to the success of the center. The new owners retained and expanded the various schools and businesses that were in the Gladish complex. Helen taught for fifteen years at the Pullman Montessori School in the building and served on the FOG board as well.

The present Gladish Community and Cultural Center is carefully maintained, is successful, and houses numerous community events, organizations, and businesses, preschools and private schools, and even a branch of Spokane Valley Community College, to name but a few. The Washington-Idaho Symphony, and Pullman Community Theater use the building for performances, as Gladish has the best 960-seat auditorium in the community (Figure IV.5.9). It is truly a positive addition to the city, one which actually serves Pullman residents. It would have been a sad loss for the entire community if it had been demolished and replaced with apartments and tract houses.

Fortunately, the old Gladish high school remains a stately edifice as a central community and cultural center. Unfortunately, the school board has had to replace its high school and build a newer one, probably with an even larger parking lot—again, more driving, traffic, sprawl and global warming. We wish the school board, the community, and the earth our best. We all need to "act locally and think globally."[17]

Town Next Door: Moscow, Idaho

In contrast to this Pullman high school story, just eight miles to the east of Pullman is Moscow, Idaho. The city of Moscow decided to expand its high school in its original central location while restoring the original historic structure, using that building as a community center for a myriad of activities.

Moscow's citizens actively participate in their historic downtown businesses, activities, annual events, and weekly farmers' markets. When visiting Moscow, it's delightful to see all ages enjoying their community center adjacent to the current high school, along with their downtown central plaza, many businesses, and restaurants within the historic core. The wide variety of people—from students to business owners and shoppers—feel invested in and proud of their city, for good reason. The preservation and adaptive use of many of their historic buildings, along with a dedication to keeping the district pedestrian-friendly, ensures its lively, vibrant character. The University of Idaho campus is within walking distance of the downtown. Many families and students enjoy the campus' tradition and historical character of both the downtown and campus (referred to locally as "town and gown").

Saving and Moving a Small Rural Town: North Bonneville, Washington

Due in part to the Pullman high school debate, Pollard Dickson decided to switch gears and study community planning at Evergreen State College. His integrated planning studio was asked to help the people of North Bonneville. The Army Corps of Engineers were planning to extend the Bonneville Dam right where the old town was located. The Corps wanted the community to disperse and avoid paying the cost of replacing the "community's human and cultural infrastructure." The town, however, did not agree and asked Pollard's class if they could help.

Through a long collaborative and participatory process (Figures IV.5.10 and IV.5.11), the town won its case and the Corps not only built a new town, but also moved a lot of the homes to the new location (Figure IV.5.12). Besides the physical infrastructure (streets, power, water, and sewer systems), the government had to replace miles of trails developed in the old town, including the exact number of trees that had been planted. The new town was also creatively planned to integrate an existing golf course. North Bonneville is now a picturesque rural town with trails connecting the town and greenways along the river (Figures IV.5.13 and IV.5.14). Thank you, Evergreen State College, Pollard Dickson, and the citizens of North Bonneville for saving the human, cultural, and environmental values of a small rural community. After his graduation, Pollard was appointed the town's planner. He and his wife are now retired and continue to live in and enjoy the town they helped move and save.

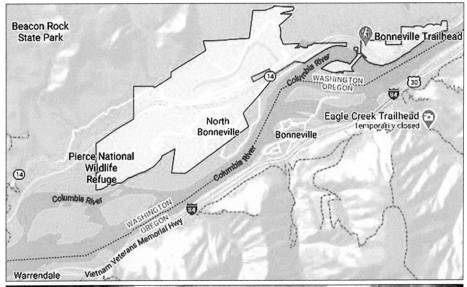

Figures IV.5.10 and IV.5.11: On the top, the old town was built in the same location as the new channel and dam just below the green marker for the Bonneville Trailhead. The new town is to the left of the new channel and north of the mighty Columbia River.
On the bottom, the town citizens participate in the selection of the new town plan. Photo courtesy of Pollard Dickson.

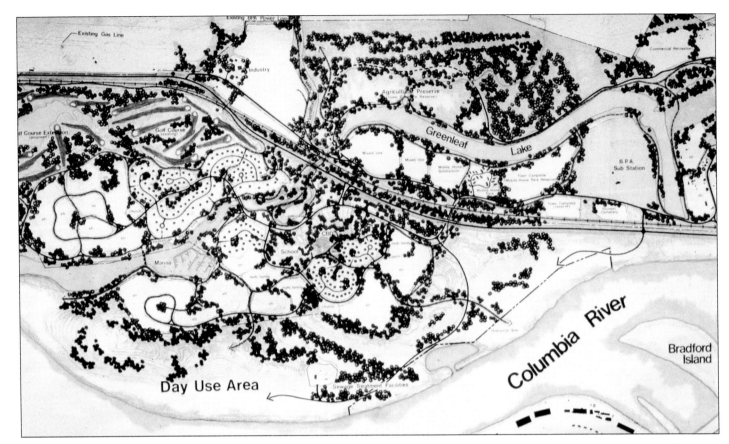

Figure IV.5.12: The new town of North Bonneville. The green areas are designed for a capacity of 600 people with an expanded area for 1,500.[18] Photo courtesy of Pollard Dickson.

Figures IV.5.13 and IV.5.14: Newly finished town hall and pedestrian trails during a town celebration.

Celebrating Community:
Restoring Pullman's City Center and the South Fork of the Palouse River

Pullman Civic Trust (PCT)

The Pullman Civic Trust has been the most active and influential citizens group in Pullman. It was formed in 1983 and has grown to over 700 members.[19] Loretta Anawalt was PCT's inspiring and long-time president. Over the years, the group has accomplished many productive citizen-based programs. Early on, it began to focus attention on Pullman's city center. As discussed earlier, the word "city" shares its root with civility and citizenship, and a city center needs to reflect the heart a of community and its culture. Unfortunately, too many business-oriented groups have been referred to as

Central Business Districts (or CBDs). This emphasis on business ignores the importance of a true civic place, where celebrating a community's history is a central part of its culture. PCT members started with sending letters to the editor of the local newspapers, offering help and encouragement to various building owners to enhance and be proud of the historic character of their buildings. The campaign was highly successful and is credited with developing Pullman's Main Street Program.

The program greatly enhanced the civic core of Pullman by improving the natural qualities of the south fork of the Palouse River that flows through the downtown. PCT created pathways

throughout the community and, through the national "Rails to Trails" program, connected to a nine-mile bike path between Pullman and Moscow, Idaho, the closest neighboring town.

Pullman's Main Street Program (MSP)

PCT was instrumental in getting state and community support for creating the Main Street Program. Established in 1985, MSP responded to what was, and still is, a challenging time for historic city centers. Downtown businesses were losing customers to the suburban sprawl that brought new shopping areas and mega-stores

Figures IV.6.1 and IV.6.2: Historic buildings convey some of the principles of the design guidelines—accent corners, display windows on the lower level, modest signage, and smaller windows above with a cornice cap. The example on the left was a car dealership; it now has retail shops below with apartments above. In the photograph on the right, the two leftmost buildings helped develop the design guidelines. The building on the far right has its historic upper facade covered up. (In the 1960s it was a common practice for store owners to cover up their original historic character facades in order to look "modern.") Behind the façade-covered front would be a more honest expression of the building's original design.

Figures IV.6.3 and IV.6.4: Two new buildings that follow the design guidelines. On the left is WSU Foundation's building, which was an important move to help revitalize downtown Pullman. The image on the right shows a structure with a fast food shop on the lower level with apartments above. The plaza is one of Pullman's vacated street auto-free zones, which leads to the river park and its extensive walkway system.

built on the perimeters of towns and cities throughout this country (with an increase in parking lots along with more traffic and pollution). The MSP goal was to refocus attention on Pullan's city center, encourage pride in its historic buildings, and help it become an active, pedestrian-friendly environment. MSP created an administrative board and hired Jim Weddell as its director. As discussed previously, Jim was a gifted WSU architecture graduate who was very interested in historic buildings and districts. Tom served on the MSP board and enjoyed Jim's leadership and collaborative/participatory approach to community development.

It is difficult to separate the many accomplishments of Pullman's MSP from PCT; the two groups have parallel emphasis and have reinforced other programs and accomplishments. They included an early downtown street banner program and the development of historic design guidelines, including signage specifications for the downtown district. With the help of PCT, the city was able to vacate a street for a traffic-free plaza. Events such as the annual National Lentil Festival brought life to the city as well as drawing people from

around the region, state, and country. Most importantly, both MSP and PCT encouraged the business community to be proud of their central location and historic center. The numbers of businesses actually increased under Jim Weddell's leadership.

The MSP design guidelines had an important effect on the way new buildings enhanced the historic character of the downtown. Bobbie Ryder, a landscape architecture professor at WSU, chaired the guidelines committee and is the current president of the PCT; Tom served on the committee, too.

The guidelines evolved through a careful examination of the historic buildings in Pullman. In general, they recommended that new buildings accent the corners of city blocks, have display windows and shops on the street level, use modest signage, have smaller windows above for offices or apartments, and have a cornice cap. Overall, they are intended to create a "sense of place" and a "variety in unity"—long-held principles of architecture and community design (Figures IV.6.1–4).

The progress PCT and MSP have made in the community over the past

thirty-plus years could fill a book. Loretta Anawalt, as PCT founding president, was instrumental in communicating PCT's vision and proposals to the Pullman city council. As PCT increased its membership and influence, many proposals received city government's support. Slowly the group took hold in the community and even influenced the elections of city council members and mayors. They proposed having a student representative on the city council and that, too, was approved.

In addition to having a supportive emphasis on the downtown district with the MSP, the PCT accomplished significant progress in changing attitudes about the historic, cultural, and environmental qualities embedded in Pullman's historic name (Three Forks) by sponsoring stream clean-up days (Figures IV.6.5 and IV.6.6). Over time, these efforts have substantially enhanced the rivers and streams, creating a downtown park with walkways along the Palouse River, and planting thousands of trees. Tom announced these programs in his classes and encouraged his students to participate in these important civic projects.

Don Heil, a friend and architecture colleague, was instrumental in proposing and building a check dam and waterfall to bring attention to the main fork running through the city center (Figure IV.6.7). PCT sponsored children's boat races in the stream, citizen workshops, surveys, and design studies to arrive at effective strategies and to increase public interest. Tom always enjoyed presenting his findings on river developments and helped other colleagues with these types of programs.

Loretta Anawalt had the inspired idea to sell leases of the land along the stream to individuals and groups. This fundraising effort was intended to raise money to protect the damaged riverbank from further erosion and to create flood control, landscaping, and trails (Figures IV.6.5–12). The people who bought the leases had to agree to landscape and maintain the property for five years, then turn it over to the city. The plan worked beautifully. We encouraged our students to raise funds, and they were able to purchase the first land lease, along with our help and in partnership with Ken Vogel, a downtown merchant. We helped each other landscape and maintain the river greenway. Our family planted the first two trees in the new riverfront park. The initiative was one of those keystone community events that made a significant change to the quality and character of the city center—but, even more so, in the personal investment and commitment to our civic community.

PCT provided the leadership in creating an eight-mile trail along an abandoned rail line (under the "Rails to Trails" Federal Program) along the streams between Pullman and Moscow, Idaho (Figure IV.6.13). Moscow, home to the University of Idaho, has a similar pro-active citizenry dedicated

Figures IV.6.5 and IV.6.6: Top, students are cleaning up the area and planting trees along the river, 1975. On the bottom, the results of those efforts are evident years later, with pathways and pedestrian bridges linking the community to the natural environment. Photos courtesy of Ken Carper.

to preserving and enhancing the historic downtown and environmental characteristics.

We remember like it was yesterday: the work and words of Nancy Mack, a PCT member who headed the trail subcommittee. At the dedication of the completed eight-mile trail, she said she was motivated by her children, giving them a safe place to ride their bikes and enjoy

the river and the Palouse countryside. She stated that she had started this effort when they were young, but now that it's finished, they were grown, married, and living in other communities.

Another important citizen-based organization is the Palouse-Clearwater Environmental Institute (PCEI). Their goal is to "connect people, place, and community." Since 1986, their programs

Figure IV.6.7: The sculptural check dam, designed and built by Don Heil, during the children's boat races.

River watersheds. Like rivers, PCEI transcends and interconnects governmental and political boundaries.

MSP, PCT, and PCEI actions have a timeless vision to improve our shared community and environment. With PCEI leadership, the highly successful "rails to trails" development was extended another fifteen miles east to Troy, Idaho. PCT is working to extend it to Colfax, Washington, fifteen miles north of Pullman. PCT has also extended the trails system throughout Pullman, along the three forks that flow through the community, the Palouse countryside, and around WSU.

Another notable major change has been the MSP and PCT's influence on the university. The WSU administrators decided to move their Foundation offices to downtown (Figure IV.6.3), and for a time they moved their bookstore off campus. The PCT analysis showed the "Bookie" had become more like a department store, with annual sales greater than all the struggling shops in the downtown city center combined. Re-established as a textbook-only store in a different location, the Bookie contributed to downtown Pullman's livelihood through growth in pedestrian activity.

have encouraged sustainable living, provided experiential learning, and offered opportunities for serving in our community, while actively protecting and restoring our natural resources.[20] PCEI has restored miles of streams and waterways throughout the Palouse, including the three forks/streams that flow through Pullman. Tom Lamar has been its director since its conception and when we lived in Pullman, we were active participants in their tree-planting programs. Tom also enjoyed serving on the board for a number of years, along with other Pullman and Moscow members. PCEI and PCT have actively collaborated on projects over the years. In addition to having restored many miles of waterways on the Palouse, with citizen and student participation they have planted thousands of trees every year and accomplished many additional environmental programs. They have an extensive environmental learning center in Moscow, which serves communities throughout the Palouse and Clearwater

Figures IV.6.8 and IV.6.9: On the left, citizens and students gather to purchase a lease on the land along the river and its trail and redevelopment. The land parcel people are standing on is the parcel the architecture group and Ken Vogel "purchased." On the right, the auctioneer and the recorder stand in front of the Palouse river.

Figures IV.6.10, IV.6.11, and IV.6.12: The degraded riverbank in 1980 (left) and the river today (right). On the left are Tom and our son Jon helping to build the pathway (shown completed in middle photo).

All these programs and projects helped change the attitude about civility and the quality of historic city centers. As illustrated in Figure IV.6.3, WSU helped by constructing a new building to house the WSU Foundation offices downtown. The building, although new, follows the historic guidelines and merges well into the character of the historic downtown. Other developers followed suit and have renewed historic buildings and even created housing and offices on the second and third levels—further enriching the diversity and 24-hour life

Figure IV.6.13: The celebration of the opening of the eight-mile "Rails to Trails" bike path between Pullman and Moscow, ID.

of the city. As stated before, personal involvement, perseverance, and patience can be the avenue to fun and success.

The National Lentil Festival

We conclude this chapter with some fun—Pullman's annual National Lentil Festival (Figures IV.6.14–18). It was started after PCT's analysis of what is truly unique about Pullman and the Palouse. The surrounding Palouse region is proud of its fertile land, farms, and productivity, especially wheat and lentils. Pullman established the Festival in 1989, and it generally draws about 4,000 participants locally and from throughout the country. The Festival celebrates the protein-rich "super food," the lentil (a legume). Lentils are an important food for starving populations in many places throughout the world. Farmers on the Palouse grow 25 percent of the nation's lentils. The Festival has a cooking contest (lentil brownies and cakes from lentil flour are favorites), a parade, a 5K run, a brew-fest, a variety of food trucks, local business displays, and music.

Figures IV.6.14, IV.6.15, IV.6.16, IV.6.17, and IV.6.18: Top, left to right: 2012 poster (selected from an annual design contest) and the participants enjoying the festival and the chili. Bottom, left to right: Volunteers at the world's largest chili pot offering free bowls of delicious and nutritious lentil chili to the crowds.[21]

NOTES

1. https://en.wikipedia.org/wiki/Rudolph_Weaver

2. Alumni Association fact sheet received from the Center, circa 2004.

3. Information from a plaque below the bell. The moving of the bell was funded by the class of 1948 in recognition of the WSU Alumni Association Centennial.

4. Tithe barns were large barns in which a parish's agricultural tithe from farmers was stored.

5. "*Pullman Herald: The First 100 Years, 1888-1988*." Special edition of *Pullman Herald*, April 11, 1988, Pullman, Washington, 17.

6. Information plate in the barn

7. https://www.artisanbarn.org/story-of-the-barn.php

8. Information plate in the barn

9. https://www.artisanbarn.org/story-of-the-barn.php

10. https://www.artisanbarn.org/

11. https://www.facebook/com/DahmenBarn/photos/a.274239229321444415377707819/?type=1&theater

12. Springen, K. "Building Atmosphere." *Newsweek* (New York, NY, 14 September 2005).

13. http://www.nicksarillo.com/2015/principles-practices-of-integral-sustainability-part-1/

14. https://www.workman.com/authors/jack-a-sobon

15. http://ntserver1.wsulibs.wsu.edu/masc/finders/cg689.htm

16. http://ntserver1.wsulibs.wsu.edu/masc/finders/cg689.htm

17. https://en.wikipedia.org/wiki/Think_globally,_act_locally

18. https://en.wikipedia.org/wiki/North_Bonneville,_Washington

19. https://www.pullmancivictrust.org/about_us

20. https://pcei.org/

21. https://en.wikipedia.org/wiki/National_Lentil_Festival

Robert Hubner, WSU Photo Services

CHAPTER V

CONSPECTUS

Barns, Buildings, and Communities that Help Sustain Our Cultural Heritage

The lyrics of the song "Circle" provide an uplifting sentiment of the ways in which circles represent how we are all connected to one another:

And this circle just goes on and on…Connecting our humanity; joining me to you and you to me…Seasons keep spinning on the wheel of time…Love and learn and change and grow…And this circle touches everyone as it crosses every boundary underneath the sun…Yes, this circle just goes on and on and on.[1]

●

Creating this book has been an adventure and a memorable experience. We use the word "conspectus" (instead of conclusion), as the following are our concluding remarks in perspective of our journey. We have enjoyed meeting and talking to the proud owners of the barns; many were grandchildren, sometimes great-grandchildren, of the original barn owners. They have been so kind in sharing information and letting us photograph these unique cathedrals to our cultural heritage. We are also indebted to the Washington State Department of Archeology and Historic Preservation (DAHP) for their help and extensive documentation.

This book has been created as a record of our 60-plus years of interest in the beauty of rural landscape and especially round barns. We have endeavored to accurately recall and relate our past conversations with owners. It was our goal to document our findings, provide an accurate and up-to-date inventory of the historic round barns of Washington, and encourage owners to maintain and preserve the unique qualities their barns contribute to our state's

rural history and its landscape. Those findings required our recognition of, and involvement in, further community-based projects in preservation and adaptive reuse to help preserve our heritage and promote sustainability.

Our journey began in earnest when we started researching and photographing fourteen barns in the 1960s. Unfortunately, four of those have since disappeared. We read many articles that concluded there were only eight to ten round barns in the entire state. The DAHP barn inventory lists fourteen. As you have seen in this volume, we have discovered and documented twenty-one barns, but we cannot help but wonder if there might be a few more hiding out there, particularly in light of our most recent accidental discovery of the Gallaher Round Barn that burned down in the 1920s and its related octagonal "house of sixteen gables." Of those twenty-one round barns we have documented, seven have disappeared. Considering our young ages of 80 years-plus, we wanted to document and share our love affair with these amazing structures before more disappear (or we do).

During the writing of this journey, we began with the historic development of round barns—the functional and structural efficiency for the family farm. We summarized our knowledge and research on the unique round barns in Washington state, honoring the oldest first and also including those that have disappeared. We presented several ways in which other round and rectangular barns have been saved and adaptively reused. We ultimately concluded with ways our long-time hometown of Pullman, Washington, has revitalized its historic buildings, city center, and downtown riverfront. All are enhanced by special people with the will and wisdom to save—even move and reconstruct—barns and buildings to enrich and sustain our rural culture along with its landscape and communities.

Here today, hopefully not gone tomorrow: Washington is very fortunate to still have fourteen of its twenty-one round barns. We cannot overemphasize how important it is to retain these barns as part of our culture and agricultural heritage, or how significant preserving them will be for future generations.

As society changes, so do aspects of the built and natural environments we inhabit. Dynamic changes in the size and ownership of farms (agribusiness vs. family farms) have become increasingly prevalent and diminish the usefulness of these historic buildings in their traditional roles. The functions, technologies, and costly maintenance of large-scale wooden construction collectively make historic barns all the more vulnerable and, therefore, all the more valuable and critical to save. Fortunately, our state has funding through DAHP to provide a competitive matching grant program to financially help preserve and rehab them.

As emphasized earlier, it is important and highly advisable to contact the owners of any barns you may want to visit before traveling to see them, especially if you want to photograph their striking interior spaces and experience their awesome structures. We made that mistake many times.

Finally, the unfortunate pressures of urban, exurban, and suburban sprawl, along with the related auto-driven lifestyles as well as the expansion of agribusiness farming practices that are overtaking the small family farm, are consuming land and resources at a dramatic rate. These changes place extreme pressure on the rural environment, their historic structures, and most importantly, the sustainability of our shared planet, Earth. We hope this book will increase the curiosity of some readers to investigate the possibility of additional round barns out there and to add their discoveries to the existing inventory. We also hope our words will encourage the preservation and reanimation of these unique cultural icons to help sustain the inspirational beauty of the rural barns, historic buildings, towns, and landscape for generations to come.

To conclude, one of our favorite John Muir quotes directs us to the harmony and inspiration of human-environmental interactions:

> Climb the mountains and get their good tidings. Nature's peace will flow into you as sunshine flows into trees. The winds will blow their own freshness into you, and the storms their energy, while cares will drop away from you like the leaves of Autumn.[2]

To that advice, we add our own:

> Ponder the rural landscape and be inspired by the beauty of its natural and human qualities (especially round forms).

Notes

1. From the song "Circle," lyrics and music by Jud Friedman and Cynthia Weil

2. John Muir, *The Mountains of California*, New York: The Century Co., 1894.

ADDITIONAL RESOURCES ON ROUND BARNS

Hanou, John T. *A Round Indiana: Round Barns in the Hoosier State*. Purdue University Press, 1993. Second edition, 2020.

Hazeltine, Luella, and Deb Schense. *Barns Around Iowa: A Sampling of Iowa's Round Barns*. Penfield Books, 2008.

Jackson, Jacqueline Dougan. *The Round Barn: A Biography of An American Farm* (four volumes). Self-published, 2013.

Jackson, Jacqueline Dougan. *More Stories from the Round Barn*. TriQuarterly Press, 2002.

Jackson, Jacqueline Dougan. *Stories from the Round Barn*. TriQuarterly Press, 2000.

Kanfer, Larry and Alaina Kanfer. *Barns of Illinois*. University of Illinois Press, 2009.

Kroeger, Robert. *Round Barns of America: 75 Icons of History*. Acclaim Press, 2022.

Soike, Lowell J. *Without Right Angles: The Round Barns of Iowa*. Penfield Books, 1991.

Triumpho, Richard. *Round Barns of New York*. Syracuse University Press, 2004.

Twiggs, John, director. "Keeping the Barn." Montana PBS, 2020. https://www.montanapbs.org/programs/keepingthebarn/

Wisconsin Round Barn and Other Round Structures List, updated by Dale Travis,
    http://www.dalejtravis.com/rblist/rbwi.htm

Robert Hubner, WSU Photo Services

The beautiful colors and curves of the Palouse wheat fields.

INDEX

ABOUT THE AUTHORS

The authors have been interested in round barns, reanimating rural buildings and communities for some 60 years. They are avid world travelers including a year in Afghanistan when Tom was awarded a Fulbright teaching at Kabul University and Helen taught at an international primary school. Now they reside in the Pacific Northwest and both volunteer at IslandWood, an outdoor school with national recognition for its outdoor programs and contemporary sustainable design.

Helen taught pre-school for 35 years including being a directress/educator at a Montessori school. She received her degree in design and child development as well as graduate studies for her Montessori certification in London. She was active in community education serving on curriculum commissions for our public schools and was involved in the YWCA program "Today's Children – Our Nation's Future" (a grant from the Washington Humanities Commission). She was a board member of a community organization that was instrumental in saving a major historic building (now an active community center), taught English as a second language and is a skilled editor.

Tom is an architect and professor emeritus, having taught theory, design, and planning with an emphasis on sustainability for 40 years, including five programs in London. He helped create and coordinated a unique all-university course involving all the design and planning disciplines—The Built Environment (at times the enrollment exceeded 300). Based on this unique course, he co-authored and edited two interdisciplinary books on the Built Environment, numerous chapters in other books, and served on planning and design commissions. He collaborated with two other colleagues, and they were one of three internationally to receive a gold metal at the UN Habitat Conference for their work on sustainable development.

Pam Overholtzer, our editor, practiced Interior Design with emphasis on historic preservation for over 20 years prior to earning a Masters in Architecture at the University of Idaho. During that time, she taught architecture classes while tutoring in the English department. She worked to establish a downtown historic district in Moscow, Idaho, and served on the Historic Preservation Commission. Upon graduating with the AIA Medal of Excellence, she continued teaching and practicing sustainable architecture with a focus on adaptive reuse. She was design and production manager for a professional international journal and was editor on several books on architecture, including work on *The Built Environment* with Wendy McClure and Tom Bartuska.

Shelly Hanks, WSU Photo Services